Systematic Methods for Analyzing Culture provides a ti͏ tion and analysis. This user-friendly book will engage students and scholars... guides are an excellent resource, while the book overall offers much, much more.
— **Leon Anderson**, Professor Emeritus, Department of Sociology, Social Work, and Anthropology, Utah State University, USA

At last—a practical guide for teaching and learning systematic methods for collecting and analyzing cultural data. Professors who've wanted to teach this course but held back because they needed a text for their students to follow now have that book.
— **H. Russell Bernard**, Director, Institute for Social Science Research, Arizona State University, USA

This is an excellent book. It provides very clear explanations of a variety of important methods, and at the same time provides specific guidance on how to use them on real data. It also presents very nice examples of how results using these methods were interpreted in published studies. I heartily recommend the book.
— **Steve P. Borgatti**, Chair and Professor, Department of Management, Gatton College of Business and Economics, University of Kentucky, USA

If you put off trying to understand how culture affects health in your research because it seemed outside of your field, you no longer have an excuse. Clear, readable (and sometimes humorous!) explanations of theory with step-by-step methods make this the perfect resource for those new to cultural analysis.
— **Michelle Carras**, Practicing Public Health Research Associate, USA

This book is an exciting contribution that will be useful to researchers at multiple levels who are incorporating cognitive methods for the study of culture into their study designs: professionals, faculty, graduate students, and advanced undergraduates. As a comprehensive and detailed step-by-step guide, it makes decades of innovation in ethnographically grounded quantitative methods far more understandable, and is unlike anything else available on the market. This will be an especially important practical tool for teaching and mentorship.
— **Jason A. DeCaro**, Professor, Department of Anthropology, The University of Alabama, USA

This book is an excellent resource for researchers interested in examining human cultures for a broad array of different academic fields. The guide is also a great tool for teaching research methods. The authors use clear examples to uniquely guide readers step-by-step through the processes of data collection and analysis.
— **Michael Gavin**, Professor, Department of Human Dimensions of Natural Resources, College of Natural Resources, Colorado State University, USA

Dengah, Snodgrass, and colleagues have done a remarkable job pulling together a diverse and powerful and set of methods for analyzing cultural phenomena. Perhaps more impressively, they give the reader clear, step by step instructions for how to actually carry out the analyses—a set of skills that heretofore one needed a secret handshake to access. This will be a goldmine for researchers and students.
— **Craig Hadley**, Professor, Department of Anthropology, Emory University, USA

Continuing a long legacy of cognitive anthropology's contribution to anthropological theory and methods, Systematic Methods for Analyzing Culture: A Practical Guide provides readers with a clear roadmap in applying contemporary cognitive anthropology theories and methods to their ethnographic research through innovative data sets and practice problems.

— **Douglas W. Hume**, Chair and Associate Professor, Department of Sociology, Anthropology, and Philosophy, Northern Kentucky University, USA

I've longed for a book like this, which presents the cognitive science behind cultural models in a clear and accessible way, and then offers practical methods to identify those models. These methods do not replace participant observation (as the authors point out) but they do enhance them. They provide, in effect, a way of crystalizing what ethnographers do into findings that are understandable across many disciplines. This is a very teachable and useful book.

— **Tanya Marie Luhrmann**, Professor, Department of Anthropology, Stanford University, USA

A well-crafted practical textbook to help master the research tools necessary to assess cultural sharing and get better acquainted with the most relevant anthropological theoretical frameworks.

— **Kateryna Maltseva**, Chair and Associate Professor, Department of Sociology, National University of Kyiv-Mohyla Academy, Ukraine

This book represents an essential, rigorous, and timely contribution to the social sciences, providing the reader with step-by-step practical guidance on how to collect and analyze cultural data in a sound way.

— **Halley M. Pontes**, Lecturer and Researcher, School of Psychological Sciences, University of Tasmania, Australia

Anthropologists who approach their craft as science will find this book a welcome addition as there are currently only a small number of practical guides. The topics covered by this book are exactly those that are increasingly used in both academic and applied anthropological research.

— **Christopher McCarty**, Professor, Department of Anthropology, University of Florida, USA

This book is a 'compass' in the methodological maze of collecting and interpreting cultural data in our globalized world. It will safely guide you to your destination!

— **Vasileios Stavropoulos**, Senior Lecturer of Clinical Psychology, Victoria University, Australia

This long-overdue 'how to' manual provides clear, step-by-step instructions for researchers wishing to robustly incorporate cultural beliefs and behaviors into qualitative and quantitative research. It is an unprecedented contribution to psychological anthropology (and beyond).

— **Lesley Jo Weaver**, Associate Professor, Department of International Studies, University of Oregon, USA

Culture matters, now more than ever when humanity must negotiate difference to meet pressing challenges. Methods matter, too, and this invaluable handbook empowers users to open the black box of culture and probe specific lived worlds through their constituent concepts, logics and dynamics. An essential source that is certain to advance our understanding of a phenomenon universal among humans, but endlessly varied in its forms.

— **Carol M. Worthman**, Professor, Department of Anthropology, Emory University, USA

This book brings together, in a practical step-by-step guide, new and old methods for studying culture. It is an essential resource for learning a range of approaches for systematically analyzing cultural data.

— **Amber Wutich**, Professor, School of Human Evolution and Social Change, Arizona State University, USA

The idea that social scientific research is either qualitative or quantitative is mistaken. Cultural data can be collected, studied, and analyzed systematically, and this volume shows that in the most comprehensive way.

— **Dimitris Xygalatas**, Associate Professor, Departments of Anthropology and Psychological Sciences, University of Connecticut, USA

Systematic Methods for Analyzing Culture

Systematic Methods for Analyzing Culture is a practical manual that provides step-by-step instruction for collecting and analyzing cultural data. This compact guide explains complex topics in straightforward and practical terms, via research examples, textual and visual software guides, and hands-on exercises.

Through each chapter's introductory examples, the manual illustrates how socially learned knowledge provides group members with shared understandings of the world, which allow for mutually intelligible interactions. The authors then carefully walk readers through the process of eliciting those socially learned, shared, and thus cultural representations of reality, which structure the thinking and practice of individuals inhabiting social groups. Specifically, the book shows how researchers can elicit such thought and behavior via methods such as free lists, pile sorts, cultural consensus and consonance analysis, textual analysis, and personal network research.

The book will help both undergraduate and graduate students identify ways to unpack the "black box" of culture, which may be absent or given only cursory attention within their training and respective fields. The book's clear and systematic step-by-step walkthroughs of each method will also encourage more established researchers, educators, and practitioners—from diverse fields and with varying levels of experience—to integrate techniques for assessing cultural processes into their research, teaching, and practice.

H.J. François Dengah II, PhD, is an Associate Professor of Anthropology at Utah State University.

Jeffrey G. Snodgrass, PhD, is Professor of Anthropology at Colorado State University.

Evan R. Polzer is a practicing social scientist at the University of Colorado's Department of Emergency Medicine.

William Cody Nixon is a current MA student at Colorado State University's Department of Anthropology and Geography.

Systematic Methods for Analyzing Culture
A Practical Guide

H.J. François Dengah II,
Jeffrey G. Snodgrass,
Evan R. Polzer and
William Cody Nixon

Routledge
Taylor & Francis Group

LONDON AND NEW YORK

First published 2021
by Routledge
2 Park Square, Milton Park, Abingdon, Oxon OX14 4RN

and by Routledge
52 Vanderbilt Avenue, New York, NY 10017

Routledge is an imprint of the Taylor & Francis Group, an informa business

© 2021 H.J. François Dengah II, Jeffrey G. Snodgrass, Evan R. Polzer and William Cody Nixon

British Library Cataloguing-in-Publication Data
A catalogue record for this book is available from the British Library

Library of Congress Cataloging-in-Publication Data
Names: Dengah, H.J. François, author. | Snodgrass, Jeffrey G., author. | Polzer, Evan R., author.
Title: Systematic methods for analyzing culture: a practical guide / H.J. François Dengah II,
Jeffrey G. Snodgrass, Evan R. Polzer and William Cody Nixon.
Description: New York : Routledge, 2021. |
Includes bibliographical references and index.
Identifiers: LCCN 2020032313 (print) | LCCN 2020032314 (ebook) |
ISBN 9780367551520 (hardback) | ISBN 9780367551513 (paperback) |
ISBN 9781003092179 (ebook)
Subjects: LCSH: Social sciences—Research. | Culture—Research. |
Cognition. | Research—Methodology.
Classification: LCC H62 .D3956 2021 (print) |
LCC H62 (ebook) | DDC 306.072/1—dc23
LC record available at https://lccn.loc.gov/2020032313
LC ebook record available at https://lccn.loc.gov/2020032314

ISBN: 978-0-367-55152-0 (hbk)
ISBN: 978-0-367-55151-3 (pbk)
ISBN: 978-1-003-09217-9 (ebk)

Typeset in Times
by codeMantra

Visit the eResources: www.routledge.com/9780367551513

Contents

List of figures

List of tables

Foreword

Of the several features that distinguish anthropology as a field of study, the emphasis on the concept of culture is probably most important. Furthermore, there is a distinctive perspective on culture that is rooted in the thinking of Franz Boas and his students (particularly Edward Sapir), which grew and matured throughout the 20th century. This is, simply put, to see the world as others see it. More precisely, to understand people in their own social context, we must discover those categories that they themselves use to construct their reality, and we must describe their lives employing those categories.

In cultural anthropology, this came to be termed an "emic" perspective. Clearly this is a very general goal of research. The utility of an emic perspective was bolstered by the development of theory in cognitive anthropology, and especially a theory of cultural models. Cultural models are, in succinct terms, skeletal and stripped-down mental representations of some cultural domain of interest, a domain itself being some topic that is important enough to people that they talk about it. Cultural models are used in everyday life by people to *think* about things, and they think about these things in terms of the categories they have learned in society and that they share with others.

At this point, it gets more complicated. Eliciting the models that construct the world for people is no simple task, mainly because those models are so implicit and pervasive that we literally don't think about them. For us, the models are simply our reality and we have little cognizance of just how arbitrary they are (e.g., what genius came up with the notion that a university semester should be 15 weeks long?).

This is a question of method. How can we reliably elicit the categories that people use to describe their world, with some assurance that these are indeed the terms they employ. That is, are they valid descriptors? Happily, in the past 40 years or so, there has developed a suite of methods that have proven quite effective in studying cultural models and how they are shared and distributed in a social group. These include ways of eliciting terms and describing how they are linked; analytic methods that assist us in discovering the most important features of cultural models that people attend to; quantitative methods that test the degree to which cultural models are shared and distributed; qualitative methods that help to better contextualize the models; and, a way of assessing accurately the degree to which individuals actually incorporate the cultural into their own lives.

This theory and method have excited much interest in anthropology, as well as in public health, education, psychology, evolutionary biology, and other fields. What has limited its adoption, however, is the lack of a text that guides the interested student or researcher through the theory and method, and especially provides a concrete, step-by-step guide to actually using them.

Thankfully, François Dengah and Jeff Snodgrass, along with their students Evan Polzer and William Nixon, with *Systematic Methods for Analyzing Culture*, have done just that. Students or researchers who wish to incorporate this perspective into their own work are provided with all the tools they need in this brief but comprehensive book. Do not be deceived by how compact it is. Everything is in it that you need to start your work, right down to exercises that will guide you through the use of software for both qualitative and specialized quantitative analyses. Nor do you need to learn any arcane jargon or specialized statistics (although as you learn the power of the perspective and see its results in your own work you will be stimulated to further develop your understanding). The tools you need not only to start but to carry on your work at a sophisticated level are all here.

François, Jeff, and I go back a long way, and my own research over the past 20 years or so has been influenced by their work and their thinking. I am a couple of generations ahead of them in anthropology, having come up in the 1970s under the guidance of Pertti J. ("Bert") Pelto, author of one of the early comprehensive research methods textbooks in cultural anthropology and a tireless advocate for greater methodological awareness in the field (who, at the age of 95, just published a history of mixed-methods research). I am also a long-time colleague and friend of H. Russell ("Russ") Bernard, whose research textbook in cultural anthropology came out in the 1980s and is now in its sixth edition. The late 20th century in anthropology involved, among other things, a great deal of soul-searching regarding the logical status of anthropological descriptions. Could the lone ethnographer, based on months residing in a community, generate a valid description of culture? In response, some anthropologists downplayed the importance of a scientific validity in favor of a post-modernist-flavored interpretivist approach. Bert, Russ, and others, on the other hand, emphasized how incorporating clear, reliable, replicable methods into ethnographic fieldwork could help to resolve questions about the truth-value of our work.

I see François, Jeff, and their co-authors continuing and extending the tradition of Bert and Russ, exploring how the work of anthropologists and related social scientists can be enhanced by a focus on solid and systematic research methods. Furthermore, the theory and method that they explicate in this book cuts right to the core of the anthropological prime directive: to describe the world in the terms that people themselves use to construct it, and to locate individuals in that space of meaning. Providing this resource for a wider audience to learn and use this theory and these methods is sure to have a positive effect on research in anthropology and related fields.

William W. Dressler
Tuscaloosa, Alabama
June 24, 2020

Acknowledgments

François

This book is the product of many years of instruction and collaboration with numerous individuals. There are a few people that have been particularly formative in the creation of this book my (François') perspective. First, *muitíssimo obrigado* to Bill Dressler for his continuing mentorship and friendship. Studying under Bill has fundamentally shaped my thinking about methods, and about the role of culture in shaping our lives. Much of Chapters 5 and 6 are directly influenced by his own thinking on these subjects. I also want to express my appreciation to Kathy Oths and Kate Browne for their methods instruction at earlier points in my education. Their advice and recommendations continue to echo in my head. I would be remiss not to thank the students of my Collaborative Anthropological Research Lab who inspired me to make the first hand-outs and powerpoints that would later become the basis of this book. In particular, I want to acknowledge Elizabeth Bingham-Thomas, Erica Hawvermale, and Essa Temple. The original core of the group—they are the future of the field and this book was written with them in mind. Finally, I want to thank Anna Cohen and Rafa for their support and patience during the creation of this book, particularly during the "unique" time we find ourselves living in.

Jeff

In this book, I (Jeff) stand on the shoulders of methods giants. As I'm already tall, that gives me quite a perspective on things. So, first and foremost, I'd like to thank the methodologists (and theorists) who have developed and promoted the tools and perspectives featured in this book. That includes folks like Russ Bernard, Steve Borgatti, Roy D'Andrade, Bill Dressler, Lance Gravlee, Chris McCarty, and Amber Wutich. Writing a teaching book got me thinking about the influence so many amazing teachers have had on my life, from my time at Tulakes Elementary School to McCallie to Vanderbilt to the University of California, San Diego. Let me simply thank here a (relatively speaking) more recent group of educators, my dissertation committee members, each of whom has been an important mentor to me and whose influence resonates throughout this book (though they might not all see it): Freddy Bailey, Roy D'Andrade, Tanya Luhrmann, and Michael Meeker. On the flipside, I thank the students who have joined me in my methodological excursions, many of whom have been research collaborators, and teachers of a kind in their own right. I won't name them here, as they wouldn't all fit, though some important ones feature as co-authors in my publications and can be found in this book's references. I'd also like to thank a handful of long-term research collaborators, from whom I've learned so much: Mohan Lal Advani, Yuvraj Singh Jhala, Mike Lacy, and Chakrapani Upadhyay. And I similarly appreciate the many research participants who have joined me in my various projects—thank you, without you, none of this would have been possible. Finally, a note of appreciation to my family, friends, partners, and colleagues who have made my life's journey such a positive one.

Evan

Acknowledgments are always a bit difficult—it's a hard task to pinpoint individuals to praise when so much of who we are is shaped by innumerable people throughout our lives. To start, I'd (Evan) like to give thanks to my family. They've always encouraged a curiosity to understand more about how the world works, why people are the way they are, and to keep learning more about not just others, but also myself. They've been foundational in my spirit throughout this book and my life. Next, I'd like to give credit to my collaborators in this work. This has truly been a learning experience for all of us; this process has enabled me to further hone my anthropological training and feel more confident in my abilities as a practicing social scientist. As a final note, I would like to extend my gratitude to various other instructors, researchers, and collaborators who've instilled upon me mantras, methods training, and other professional skills. These include those from Colorado State University's Department of Anthropology & Geography, the University of Colorado's Department of Emergency Medicine, and countless others who I've met through grad seminars, lectures, sponsored events, professional development meetings, conferences, and more. May the lessons detailed in this work inspire the same curiosity that has inspired me.

Cody

As a junior author and current MA student, much of the work done on my (Cody's) end was built on the back of my mentor and co-author, Jeff Snodgrass, and with the help of my co-authors Francois Dengah and Evan Polzer. This was my first time embarking on such an ambitious collaborative academic endeavor, and the teamwork within our group was what really allowed my contributions to flourish. In addition, my parents' unwavering support and pride has continuously given me the strength and confidence I've needed to take each challenge head-on. I'd like to also thank all of my instructors and colleagues at Colorado State University (CSU), who have given me the tools to become a better anthropologist, and who have always pushed me to transform my curiosities into something worthwhile. CSU's Department of Anthropology and Geography has become my new home, and I'd like to extend a heartfelt thank you to everyone I've had the pleasure of working with there. Each of them has aided in my growth as a budding anthropologist. I hope that this book will allow others to pursue their academic inquiries through a new perspective, just as I have learned to do.

1 Introduction

This book presents a practical step-by-step guide to conducting research within the cognitive anthropological "cultural models" tradition (Bennardo & De Munck, 2014; D'Andrade, 1995), which, as we approach it, intersects with cognitive linguistic analyses of socially learned "frames" of meaning (Lakoff, 2002, 2014). Loosely, cultural models (or frames) are shared and socially learned representations of reality, which structure the thinking and practice of individuals inhabiting social groups (Bennardo & De Munck, 2014). Of particular interest is how this cultural knowledge creates shared understandings of the world, which allow for mutually intelligible interactions (D'Andrade, 2006; De Munck & Bennardo, 2019). Analysis of such shared knowledge via methods like free lists and pile sorts (Chapters 3 and 4) can be used to elicit cultural models (Johnson, Weller & Brewer, 2002; Weller & Romney, 1988), which, in turn, can be analyzed via cultural consensus analysis (Chapter 5) to assess the extent to which those models are shared within a group (Romney, Weller, & Batchelder, 1986). Likewise, cultural consonance analysis (Chapter 6) is useful for researchers wishing to assess how individuals embody culture in their individual thinking and practice, especially when that match (or mismatch) might help explain human behaviors and health processes (Dressler, 2017). And, as we approach the topic, analyzing how qualitative texts are informed by underlying cultural "schemas" (also sometimes referred to as "cultural models" in the method we follow) (Quinn, 2016) (Chapter 7) can be integrated with other textual analysis traditions, including theme analysis and grounded theory (Bernard, Wutich, & Ryan, 2017), to help researchers further illuminate and theorize the causes and consequences of cultural thought and practice. Finally, personal network analysis (Chapter 8) can be used to locate shared cultural understandings within social groups and networks of interaction (McCarty, Lubbers, Vacca, & Molina, 2019), making for an even more potent "sociocognitive" framework (de Munck & Bennardo, 2019).

As one can infer from the previous paragraph's discussion, this book draws from a rich body of existing theory and method within cognitive anthropology and related fields. What we thought was missing from the field was a compact guide explaining complex topics in straightforward and practical terms, via research examples, short software guides, and hands-on exercises. Too, in order to sketch the methodological foundations of a distinctive "sociocognitive" anthropology, we found it fruitful to bring together threads more typically separated—i.e., cultural domain analysis, including the interrelated consensus and consonance frameworks, with textual and personal network analysis. In their guide on ethnography and virtual worlds, Boellstorff and his co-authors say: "we discussed the genre of a 'handbook' at length and concluded that our contribution would be a practical text to be stashed in a backpack, easily consulted, and kept 'on hand' when doing fieldwork" (Boellstorff, Nardi, Pearce, & Taylor, 2012, p. 2). We conceptualize our own book in similar terms, short and to the point, directed primarily toward research practitioners looking for practical ways to measure and assess cultural processes. The present work is theoretically grounded in its approach to cultural processes, but ultimately more of a "how to" practical handbook rather than a "what is it" conceptual kind of book. As such, we have kept this guide concise, though we provide references for those wanting to go still deeper into the methodological specifics or conceptual background of the topics covered here.

The goal of this book is to increase the accessibility of anthropological methods training to a wider audience. Anthropology, specifically cultural anthropology, is uniquely situated to address the "black box" of culture that is often absent or given only cursory attention to in other scientific disciplines. Accordingly, this book is written for a broad audience, but it is aimed particularly at advanced undergraduates and new graduate students. These students, we feel, are still developing their identities as researchers, and along with that, their theoretical and methodological orientations. An early introduction into the suite of tools offered in cultural domain and cultural model analysis will be particularly helpful in shaping the intellectual development and careers of these readers. We also think that more established researchers will find this book useful. In our dealings with fellow anthropologists and social scientists, as well as experts and stakeholders in other fields, we often find our audiences express intense interest in our methodologies, but they also perceive (incorrectly) that the barriers for these methods are too high for adoption in their own research agendas. We hope that this book and its step-by-step walkthrough of each method will go some way to assuage these fears.

We think that cognitive anthropological methods are situated in a unique place to facilitate communication across academic boundaries, and to prepare readers for applied careers with interdisciplinary collaborators. The methods discussed in this book are rooted in the so-called "mixed-methods" tradition: a combination of both qualitative and quantitative approaches. Indeed, this holistic orientation is a defining characteristic of anthropology, providing a space for qualitative, experience-driven insights, in addition to more standardized measurements and data collection techniques. What makes these cognitive anthropological methods unique, however, is their ability to operationalize and measure a concept that has often been taken for granted within anthropology—namely the phenomena of culture. By defining culture as "systems of shared knowledge" (discussed further in Chapter 2), we can construe it as interrelated "frames of meaning" or "models" of sorts, which can be analyzed and measured in a variety of ways. Beyond the theoretical value for operationalizing "culture," this has the added benefit of making the concept of culture meaningful and applicable to researchers and stakeholders in other fields (for a quick entry into the debate about the analytical utility of the culture concept, see Abu-Lughod, 2008; Aunger, 2004; for a compromise position, see Brumann, 1999). Not to diminish the role of critical, interpretive, or deconstructionist anthropology, but anthropology outside the ivory tower often requires that the research design and methods be framed in ways that communicate findings across disciplines and to various stakeholders or clients. Writing about this, applied anthropologists Paolisso and Maloney (2001) explain:

> [I]n addition to producing insightful substantive findings, the construct "cultural model" has also served us well in helping to establish rapport with scientists and environmental professionals. The construct of a "model" is central to the research paradigm of our colleagues. Our colleagues did understand that we were attempting to construct models, and although our models are not nearly as specified or predictive as say economic or ecosystem models, they do share underlying similarities in terms of their utility in capturing key relationships among cultural as well as biological variables. In the end, we appear to other scientists and environmental professionals as very scientific, which we suspect contrasts with any existing cultural understanding they have of anthropologists and anthropology…Our use of a cultural model approach, supported by well-respected and prestigious scientific funding sources, helped to legitimize us among scientists and policymakers.
>
> *(Paolisso & Maloney, 2001, pp. 44, 46)*

In our experience, as well as those of many applied and practicing anthropologists, cognitive approaches can serve as a means to convey information across disciplinary divides, particularly in cases where quantitative research is (unfairly) valued over other types of data. Further, the replicability of these methods allows for a degree of objectivity, thereby making them attractive for use by various stakeholders (Grant & Miller, 2004). Yet, it goes without saying that cultural models and cognitive methods are not a panacea, and as in any project, researchers need to use the methods most appropriate to the research questions, setting, and goals. The adoption of new methodologies must be done in conjunction with research goals, disciplinary strengths, and the expertise of researchers. For anthropologists, this means that participant-observation remains at the center of our study. As anthropologist Frank Vivelo once said, "no other methodology demands so much personally from the researcher in terms of time, labor intensity, creativity, adaptability, hardship, and commitment…(but) on the other hand, no other research techniques offer comparable personal rewards or the kind of understanding that results from…local-level immersion" (Vivelo, 1980, p. 346).

The roots of this book go back to circa 2008 when Snodgrass was Dengah's MA advisor at Colorado State University (CSU). The two of them conspired together to create an experimental ethnographic methods seminar *inside* the online game, *World of Warcraft* (for this history, see Snodgrass, 2016). Snodgrass wanted to integrate novel quantitative and qualitative methods— and more generally perspectives drawn from the behavioral sciences—into more standard ethnography based on participant-observation, which had been the foundation of his work up until then (Snodgrass, 2006, 2014). He had recently integrated survey methods into his field studies in India (e.g., see Snodgrass, Lacy et al., 2008), and was interested to further that mixed qualitative-quantitative approach to ethnographic research, and also to impart such an approach to his own students. He saw potential in cognitive anthropology, having been advised at the University of California-San Diego (UCSD) by Roy D'Andrade, a leader in that approach to anthropology. Too, he had productively employed the cultural models perspective to elicit U.S. patterns of thinking on environmental, health, and other topics, while working for the consulting firm, *Cultural Logic*, which was started by graduate school friends, Axel Aubrun and Joe Grady.[1] Dengah had a knack for mixed methods research, and quickly picked up quantitative analysis skills, including those necessary to conduct cultural consensus and consonance analyses, which were critical to the gaming and health questions we explored in that experimental methods seminar (Snodgrass, Dengah, & Lacy, 2014; Snodgrass, Dengah, Lacy, & Fagan, 2011; Snodgrass, Dengah, Lacy, & Fagan, 2013). Snodgrass often referred to Dengah as a "diamond in the rough," whose raw skill Snodgrass first spotted when Dengah was a CSU undergraduate student. In hindsight, both Snodgrass and Dengah were diamonds in the rough, with the cognitive anthropological techniques described in these pages revealing both of their deeper value and potential as scholars.

That experimental seminar started what became a fruitful long-term collaboration between Snodgrass, Dengah, and many others. The others include the two other co-authors of this handbook, Evan Polzer and Cody Nixon. Polzer is a recent MA student in Snodgrass's Ethnographic Research and Teaching Laboratory (ERTL), Nixon a current one. Over the past ten years or so, our collaborative virtual worlds research has been published in top anthropological, cultural, psychiatric, and media studies venues, with many of Snodgrass's students co-authoring on those publications (e.g., see Dengah, Snodgrass et al., 2018; Snodgrass, Bagwell et al., 2018; Snodgrass, Batchelder et al., 2017; Snodgrass, Clements et al., 2020; Snodgrass, Dengah et al., 2012; Snodgrass, Dengah et al., 2017; Snodgrass, Dengah et al., 2020). In 2013, after receiving his PhD under the tutelage of Bill Dressler at Alabama's program in biocultural medical anthropology, Dengah took a position at Utah State University (USU) in the Department of Sociology, Social Work, and Anthropology. While a PhD student at Alabama, Dengah helped Dr. Chris Lynn start his own collaborative anthropological laboratory, the Human Behavioral Ecology Research Group (HBERG). More recently, Dengah started his own Collaborative Anthropological Research Laboratory (CARL) at USU, with his own student-collaborators and co-authors in his research (Dengah et al., 2016, 2019a, b). Both Snodgrass's and Dengah's students have acquired skills that have helped them advance in their own careers. For example, Polzer is currently a practicing social scientist working at the University of Colorado's Anschutz Medical Campus. His current work focuses

---

[1] The former was a psychological anthropologist at UCSD, the latter a cognitive linguist and student of George Lakoff at UC-Berkeley. *Cultural Logic* is now the *Topos Partnership*: http://www.topospartnership.com

on developing patient decision aids and other intervention tools within the Emergency Medicine department to assist with suicide prevention efforts, utilizing patient-centered research as a means of understanding how to combat gun violence.

Snodgrass and Dengah have had success in spreading the cognitive anthropological good word among their own lab members. They each teach methods seminars at the undergraduate and graduate levels, having found similar success in those time-intensive, semester-long contexts to train their students in cognitive anthropology as an integrated theory and method. As their research has become more widely known, Snodgrass and Dengah have become aware of the demand for mixed methods cognitive anthropological methods. Much of the demand comes from researchers outside of anthropology, who wish to implement proxies for culture into their own various research endeavors. For example, Snodgrass has established ties with Montreal cultural psychiatric researchers, leading sessions on cognitive anthropological field methods at a Concordia University symposium on gaming and gambling (Summer Interactive Symposium: Research 2.0 The Virtual Stakes/Symposium Interactif d'Été: Recherche 2.0: EnJeux Du Virtuel, 2015), and over the past two summers (2018, 2019) at a McGill University Social and Cultural Neuroscience Workshop (FPR-McGill Social and Cultural Neuroscience Workshop 2019 – FPR, n.d.). Likewise, Dengah recently co-edited a special volume for the *Annals of Anthropological Practice* on collaborative research utilizing (among other things) cognitive anthropological perspectives and techniques (Copeland & Dengah, 2016).

We (Snodgrass and Dengah) are both satisfied with those efforts at methodological outreach. But we have also become aware of the challenges to communicating the practical how-to side of cognitive anthropological methods in a few hours at a workshop or in the space of journal articles pursuing multiple aims. When we went to offer advice on how to use these methods, we realized that what we considered all the necessary pieces—the theoretical grounding, the examples of best practice, the practical software guides—were spread out over a wide range of publications and guides. Much of that know-how—including the sometimes quirky ins-and-outs of software packages created by academics, such as *Visual Anthropac* (for free lists and pile sorts) (Borgatti 1992), *UCINET* (for cultural consensus analysis) (Borgatti, Everett, & Freeman 2002), and *EgoNet* (for personal network research) (McCarty, 2003)—seemed to be located largely in an oral tradition passed on from practitioner to practitioner. We had benefited from that tradition, having been taught by some of the best, e.g., Dengah in *Anthropac* by Dressler, and both of us in *EgoNet* by Chris McCarty, who wrote that program (McCarty, Lubbers, Vacca, & Molina, 2019). But we saw how such knowledge remained opaque to others outside of these networks of personal connection. We felt like we kept repeating the same information to interested others, all the while struggling to move between big-picture theory-building and practical levels of explanation. To a large extent, this book responds to both the excitement we feel at the potential of cognitive anthropological methods, and also the frustration we sometimes experience when trying to explain to those outside this sub-discipline how to practice the methodologies that have so elevated our own research. We hope this book will help researchers quickly advance in their ability to practically assess the role of culture in their various inquiries. Secondarily, we also see this as a lab manual, which we plan to employ in our own methods seminars. We hope that researchers familiar with these techniques might similarly use our handbook to impart them to their own students in similar collaborative lab contexts.

As stated, the book is directed primarily toward researchers, including those who wish to educate their own students in cognitive anthropology theory and method, or undergraduate and graduate student researchers who themselves want to independently advance in their understanding of the practice of cognitive anthropology. On the one hand, this includes cultural anthropologists wanting to include more structured and systematic proxies for cultural processes alongside their participant-observation. We view the methods we sketch as an extension of and complement to participant-observation, rather than a substitute for it. On the other hand, we also direct this handbook to non-anthropologists such as biologists, ecologists, neuroscientists, psychologists, and sociologists, who are looking for ways to integrate proxy measures for culture in their research. The methods we sketch lend themselves to identifying simple quantifiable proxies for more complex sociocultural processes—for example, what we call cultural models and frames of meaning. Such proxies can be readily assessed alongside other measures, including health biomarkers, and also assessments of environmental degradation, brain function, psychological structures and processes related to cognition, perception, motivation, personality, and the like, social networks of interaction, and much else.

To broaden the accessibility of our handbook, we have chosen to highlight examples of what we consider high-quality cognitive anthropological and cultural models research, typically by other researchers. However, we also draw from our own studies, and especially from our gaming and virtual worlds research, as this has been so critical to the growth of our methodological expertise. We present that virtual worlds research in chapter inserts, somewhat separate from the main narrative flow of each chapter, but also hopefully lending the book an overarching feeling of unity. Our focus on our virtual worlds studies might also help researchers from fields such as communication and media studies see the potential of our work for studies of the internet, new media, and the like, ideally closely linked to ethnographic studies of those contexts and processes.

Each chapter begins with a brief sketch of what we see as the potential of the specific cognitive anthropological method that is the focus of the given chapter, alongside bigger picture theoretical issues. This is followed by examples of how the technique has been used, taken, as noted, both from others' and our own research, with the latter largely in textbox inserts. From there, we present brief software guides sketching how to practically carry out the techniques that are the focus of each chapter. We conclude each chapter with practical lab exercises, with some of that found in supplementary online materials.

The next chapter (Chapter 2) presents a theoretical grounding of cognitive anthropological cultural models and cultural domain analysis. That is followed by chapters on free listing and pile sorting (Chapters 3 and 4), cultural consensus and consonance analysis (Chapters 5 and 6), a unified perspective on text analysis, centered around schema and models analysis (Chapter 7), personal network research and what we call a "sociocognitive" framework (Chapter 8), and a brief conclusion (Chapter 9).

Finally, a note on authorship. This book represents a collaborative effort, with all four of us working closely together to put it together. Weekly *Skype* meetings over several months kept us on track, along with the *Slack* software for communication and task coordination. Snodgrass wrote Chapters 1, 7, and 9, and he also contributed substantially to the writing of the other chapters and their related exercises; he provided big picture conceptualization of the book and its various moving parts, and generally managed the team's collaborative effort. Dengah led in the writing of Chapters 2, 5, and 6, and contributed importantly to the writing of the other chapters as well; he put together most of the textual and visual software guides, which in many respects are the heart of this practical guidebook to cognitive anthropology. Polzer wrote the foundation of Chapters 3, 4, and 8, while making important contributions to the introductions and case study examples of Chapters 5 and 6 in particular; he wrote and conceptualized the initial drafts of the book's practical exercises and Chapter 7's *MAXQDA* guide as well. Nixon made particularly substantial contributions to Chapter 7, as Snodgrass's research assistant during which that semester's textual analysis research was conducted, and specifically crafted initial drafts of that chapter's exercises and visual software guides; he also contributed importantly to Chapter 2 and various other parts of the book, for example, to the index, and by field-testing the practical exercises. Though we have laid out these contributions in this explicitly delineated way, each chapter's content was fundamentally shaped by a joint and ongoing conversation among the four of us, which included substantial editing and re-writing along the way.

2 Cognitive anthropology
Theoretical foundations

The cognitive anthropological approach to cultural processes deals with some of the more perplexing issues facing anthropologists and other social scientists. Namely, *what is culture? Where is it located? And how do we measure it?* Cognitive anthropology is an approach that defines culture as systems of shared knowledge necessary for individuals to interpret and function within specific environmental (natural, social, etc.) settings (Goodenough, 1994). This definition of culture represents an important departure from prior theorists who located culture solely within the minds of individuals (e.g., Ruth Benedict [1934]) or, conversely, as existing primarily between individuals in publicly communicated symbols (Geertz, 1974, 2005). By operationalizing culture as shared knowledge, culture, for cognitive and psychological anthropologists, is conceptualized as existing at *both* the individual and the aggregate interpersonal levels (De Munck, 2000). (An aside: cognitive anthropology is considered a subfield within broader psychological anthropology, which itself belongs to cultural anthropology.) Possessing common and shared understandings of the natural and social environment allows for mutually intelligible and predictable thought, behavior, and communication between individuals belonging to a group or community. If those individuals did not share cultural knowledge, even mundane behaviors such as going to the market, or waving *hello* would be impossible. How else would you be able to exchange goods, or determine if a hand gesture is a greeting or threat, if not for some sort of shared understanding between individuals?

Given that cognitive anthropological approaches to culture importantly attend to interpersonal processes of communication, it should come as little surprise that modern cognitive anthropology has its roots in linguistics. A complete recapitulation of cognitive anthropological theory and history is beyond the aims of this book, dedicated as it is to research methods. However, the interested reader is encouraged to refer to Roy D'Andrade's (1995) excellent book, *The Development of Cognitive Anthropology*, or to the more recent, *A Companion to Cognitive Anthropology*, which was edited by some of today's leaders within this field (Kronenfeld, Bennardo, de Munck, & Fisher, 2015). In this chapter, we provide a brief overview of some foundational thinking in the field, as that thought pertains directly to the methodologies described in subsequent chapters.

Before starting our brief overview in earnest, we'd say simply that one main aim and focus of cognitive anthropological research is to derive an understanding of the knowledge shared by members of a group or community about a particular *domain* (or topic), while being sensitive to individual and subcultural variation as well.[1] In essence, cognitive anthropologists try to understand the learned structures of knowledge that members of a community use to think about a particular phenomenon. And they also analyze how this thinking varies between individuals and changes over time. In cognitive anthropology, shared culture is heuristically parsed into discrete forms of knowledge: culturally learned and shared prototypes, schemas, and models, with some attention to more complex cognitive objects such as cultural theories or even ideologies and worldviews (D'Andrade, 1995). The methods in this book will show readers how to collect each one of these components of cultural knowledge (though less so for the more complex cognitive objects

---

[1] In this book, we italicize certain analytical terms, but typically only on their first substantive use or in some cases for emphasis.

such as cultural theories), and determine degrees of sharedness and variation between informants in relation to that knowledge.

THEORETICAL BACKGROUND

Much of what guides cognitive anthropology theoretically and methodologically is related to what's been called *cultural domain analysis*, or the inductive examination of a particular area of shared conceptualization or thought (D'Andrade, 1995; Johnson, Weller, & Brewer, 2002; Weller & Romney, 1988). Cognitive anthropologists aim to establish how members of groups share knowledge surrounding a particular topic, whether it be life success and failure (a focus in our own virtual worlds research; e.g., see Snodgrass, Dengah, et al., 2011, 2013; Snodgrass, Dengah, & Lacy, 2014), political thinking and attitudes on an election issue (Lakoff, 2002), or really anything that people think and communicate about. How these anthropologists reached the idea of cultural domain analysis is important to consider, so let's continue with more history.

Lounsbury and Goodenough (1964) were particularly influential in creating the foundations for cognitive anthropology (then known as ethnoscience) and what we now call "cultural domain analysis". In a series of studies, Lounsbury and Goodenough sought to identify distinctions within kinship terminologies in different societies. (Kinship terms and relationships have long been an interest within anthropology, with work dating back to the late 1800s, and are found in some of the discipline's most foundational texts.) They argued that kinship terms, such as *mother*, *father*, and *cousins* all received meaning from the relationships these categories had with other terms.[2] For example, the concept of a *cross cousin* (mother's brother's or father's sister's children) or *parallel cousin* (mother's sister's or father's brother's children) is meaningless without taking into account the gendered relationship between an individual's parents and their siblings. The point is that social organizations (such as family systems) are associated with specific categorical distinctions, what Lounsbury and Goodenough termed "idea units," used to classify human experience and thus also structure behavior (e.g., interactions between kin).

At its heart, this research was linguistic in nature, with the aim to understand how labels contained the knowledge that individuals used to structure society. (Students of anthropology may note that this is related in some ways to the Sapir-Whorf hypothesis, which postulates that language shapes thought processes (Kay & Kempton, 1984).) Indeed, D'Andrade (2001) argues that language is an essential means by which culture-as-knowledge within individuals becomes "material" (e.g., instantiated in vocalizations, writing, etc.) and thus able to be shared and transmitted between individuals. That is, some form of communication is necessary to express, develop, and acquire culture (see also Bennardo & De Munck, 2014). As D'Andrade states (2001, p. 250), "Ideas, to be communicated, need a medium—pantomime, speech, writing, or whatever."

Peeling back the linguistic connection a bit more, language, pantomime, or D'Andrade's "whatever" form of language must be organized systematically so that words (or communicative physical gestures, etc.) are discernible and interpretable (see, e.g., Jakobson, 1960; Trubetzkoy, 1969). These discernible "chunks" of sounds, movement, or ink on a page are combined to form features (the suite of sounds and vocal articulations, or hand movements in sign-language, that make up a word) possessing not just a particular sound, but also a meaning (De Saussure, 2011). Essentially, for any utterance (i.e., "sign" in semiotic-speak) to have any meaning, both the sender and receiver must have the same (or similar enough) cognitive understanding (i.e., a "signified") of what is being communicated. For example, if I write *maçã* many readers will have no idea what I

---

[2] We also italicize certain terms for emphasis, such as vocabulary used by cultural insiders, as with the kinship terms listed here.

am attempting to communicate.[3] We lack a shared understanding of this sign. However, if I write *apple*, all of sudden the anglophone readers have a clear understanding, but now I've confused the few Brazilian readers. Hence, shared knowledge is essential for the construction of a shared reality, i.e., culture.

A final note should be made about the role of linguistics in cognitive anthropological theory. In the 1960s, Kenneth Pike, an American linguist and anthropologist, laid some important groundwork for how we conceptualize language as embedded within culture (Pike, 1967). Specifically, Pike formalized the distinction between the *emic* (phonemic) and the *etic* (phonetic), two categories within linguistic theory (Pike, 1967), which also played into other linguistic theories of language and meaning (De Saussure, 2011). The emic is concerned with how languages are structured from within the culture from which they originate, and the etic from outside of that societal lens. To make this a little easier to understand, one can think of emic as related to an informed cultural insider's point of view (the *raison d'etre* of ethnography) and etic as from a more distant, outsider's point of view (D'Andrade, 1995; Dressler, 2017; Geertz, 1974). Like Pike, cognitive anthropologists contend that the best way to approach an understanding of language or culture is from an insider's—or emic—perspective. That is, unlike other disciplines that emphasize an external "truth" independent of individuals' experiences, the cognitive anthropological approach privileges the individual (in the form of personal knowledge) and individuals (in the form of shared knowledge).

Hopefully, you are now somewhat familiar with how linguistic theory has been applied to understand not just language, but other forms of shared knowledge and communication as well. Whereas Pike and other linguists focused on phonemics and thus signifiers and signifieds, and Goodenough and early ethnoscientists were concerned with idea units, today's cognitive anthropologists are more interested in cultural domains. These are not unrelated concepts, however— cultural domains can be thought of as networks of related idea units or signifiers. For example, cognitive anthropologists might take a domain like workplace responsibilities (etic) and put them through a cultural filter (emic) to understand many facets and dimensions of what comprises a group's understanding(s) of "workplace responsibilities." For us, the foundational question is: *What makes something unique in the (shared) "we-thinking" mind?* Contemporary cognitive anthropologists have many of these early linguists and anthropologists to thank for helping us arrive at this concept.

PROTOTYPES

The simplest type of cognitive knowledge is the *prototype*. A prototype refers to a generalized form, a set of characteristics which imperfectly categorize a wide range of realities (Rosch, 1999). The prototype is the easiest way by which humans cognitively order and classify their world, and it is likely based off hardwired neurological circuitry in the brain (Sapolsky, 1998). Our social and natural worlds are too varied to interpret separately each variation of a phenomenon. To compensate for this diversity, our brains are pattern-seeking devices, that classify similar phenomenon together, in order to facilitate rapid and low energy cognition (and associated behaviors) (D'Andrade, 1995). Rather than cognitively storing massive taxonomic lists of essential differences, prototypes allow people to have "generic versions of experience that remain in memory" (Strauss & Quinn, 1994). The accumulation of the average experienced characteristics of a domain (remember, cognitive anthropology's notion of domain means loosely a "topic"), through both personal experience and shared discourse, creates a standard mental representation, which allows maximum information to be stored with minimal cognitive effort. In essence, human beings think

---

[3] We also italicize foreign terms the first time we use them.

via stereotypical categories based off of individual experiences and the shared knowledge of their respective communities.

A simple thought-exercise demonstrates the power and utility of prototypes. Think of a "chair." *What is the first image that comes to your mind? What does it look like? How many legs does it have? What material is it comprised of? What color is it?* Now, assuming you are sitting as you are reading this, *how well does your mental image compare to what you are sitting on currently?* Undoubtedly, they are different, but they likely share some set of essential characteristics to qualify it as a *chair* rather than, say, a *table*. While one could technically sit on both a chair and a table, a chair is specifically designed to be sat upon by a single person (as opposed to a *bench* or a *couch*), with some sort of back support (as opposed to a *stool*). But outside those general characteristics, chairs take on a multitude of forms. Yet, our prototype chair allows us to quickly distinguish chairs from other types of furniture.

As some readers may be thinking, lots of phenomena violate prototype rules. For example, while the prototypical *bird* may be a *robin*, *sparrow*, or *black-bird*, *ostriches* and *penguins* violate some aspects of the prototype—namely, by not flying. Young children are often particularly flummoxed by these prototype transgressions. In early childhood, the socialization and enculturation processes are at their zenith (Mead & Wolfenstein, 1955), with children learning how to interact and understand their social and natural environments. Children in American culture learn that *fish* and *sharks* have certain body shapes and live in the ocean, whereas *mammals* have lots of hair and live on the land. Based on these naïve prototypes, *dolphins* and *whales* are often first incorrectly perceived to be fish by these young people, with culture thus shaping folk categorizations of the natural world (Atran, 1995; Atran & Medin, 2008).

As such, prototypes can be insightful for ascertaining taken for granted cultural stereotypes of specific phenomena. An exchange with a friend's young daughter is instructive: during the 2016 United States Presidential campaign, one of our coauthor's (Dengah) friends asked her daughter what she thought of Hillary Clinton. The daughter responded that Hillary Clinton could not be *president*, because presidents aren't women. For the young child, her prototype of what "a president is" was, among other things, gender-specific. In everyday language, we can easily identify prototype violations by looking for marked and unmarked terms. In American society, we see prototypes employed around gender and ethnicity, with terms such as act*ress,* or more explicitly: my *male* nurse, *Latino* friend, etc.

SCHEMAS

Schemas can be conceived as the skeletal structure of cognition, providing a framework for networking-related prototypes, models, and associated schematic structures (D'Andrade, 1981). As Bloch (1998, p. 6) describes them, "these 'scripts' and 'schemata' are, in effect, chunked networks of loose procedures and understandings which enable us to deal with standard and recurring situations…that are clearly culturally created." Similar to an algebraic formula in which the variables are interchangeable for a given context, schemas (or schemata, the two terms are used interchangeably) provide the means of dealing with complex situations with ease. Presenting classic work on scripts (or action schemas), Ross (2005) walks readers through the example of an American restaurant script, in which he describes action sequences related to ordering food, eating, paying, and tipping (for the original work, see Abelson, 1981; Schank & Abelson, 1975, 1977). These are in turn filled in with further models and prototypes, depending on context-specific realities, such as fast-food or fine-dining, eating alone or with others, etc.

Schemas, as such, create cognitive scaffolding which allows individuals to quickly plug in novel particularities, without focusing on the construction of the overall structure. That is, rather than memorizing or interpreting all stimuli as novel experiences, schemas provide "a general impression of the whole" and allow individuals to anticipate probable behaviors and outcomes of social interaction (Barlett in Casson, 1983, p. 430). The result is that individuals often hold aspects of the underlying structure outside of cognitive awareness—schemas are, in essence, taken for granted, implicit knowledge. Again, consider the schema for ordering food at a restaurant. *What aspects stand out to you?* Maybe you begin by looking at the menu, next telling the waiter what you want, and then finally being delivered your food. But what is absent from this narrative—or, to put it another way, what is the implied cultural knowledge? *How did you get to the restaurant? Are you sitting at a table, booth...or on the ground? What/where is the menu—on an overhead menu-board or on a piece of paper? Who actually brought you your food?* The point is that schemas are often implicit knowledge, so that they only come into awareness when violated.

Schemas differ from prototypes in an important way. While prototypes are useful in data categorization, schemas are useful for acting and reacting to this data. "A schema is not only the plan but also the executor of the plan. It is a pattern *of* action as well as a pattern *for* action" (Neisser in Casson, 1983, p. 483, emphasis in original; see also Geertz, 1977). Schemas allow us to confidently act in novel social situations—they provide a framework for our own behavior, and a map for understanding and predicting other's behavior, outside of conscious awareness. Consider the schema of a college course. There is a script that all participants follow, regardless of whether it is a math course or an anthropology course, if it is the first day of the semester or the last. Students, without being explicitly told, enter the classroom and sit at desks that face all in one direction (the classroom script is also the focus of classic work in cognitive science; see Schank & Abelson, 1975). The professor stands at one end of the room which the students are facing. When the professor is talking, students are (usually) silent and attentive, taking notes. Schemas are only useful if they are shared and each party is convinced that others also share in this knowledge. Again, this schema only comes into conscious awareness when there is a violation of it: the professor does not show up for class; students are disruptive; the professor conducts class sitting on the floor. In cases where the schema breaks down, social behavior becomes less predictable, thereby requiring more focused cognition. A distinguishing feature of schemas, as compared to models (discussed below), are that schemas are cognitive representations that are small and simple enough to be held in working memory and clearly articulated (D'Andrade, 1995; Dressler, 2017).

MODELS

Cultural models, the unit of investigation in most cognitive anthropological work, are more abstract and complex than schemas (D'Andrade, 1995). They are generally composed of multiple schemas, prototypes, and even other models. Since they are so complex, models generally cannot be fully retained within working memory. Rather, they are implicit knowledge that nevertheless requires conscious reflection and active construction and reasoning. And like schemas, cultural models, by definition, need to be shared and distributed among a population to function.

Cultural models direct what D'Andrade (1992, p. 39) has called "master motives," as they collectively organize aspects of worldview, identity, motivations and the like. As such, cultural models often manifest as *habitus*, which is a fancy way of saying recurrent behavioral patterns (or habits, get it?) that are reified as an external force (Bourdieu, 1977; Handwerker, 2002; Strauss & Quinn, 1997). And because they are shared, cultural models (as well as schemas) are self-motivating. Functional social interactions are predicated on the assumption of shared knowledge within a group—that is, the ideas that others are also operating from the same knowledge system. (Adherence and deviance to cultural models is something that we will explore in Chapters 5 and 6 on cultural consensus and consonance.)

Bill Dressler has spent much of his career identifying Brazilian cultural models of material lifestyle, a good family life, food, and others (for a good summary of three decades of this work, see Dressler, 2017). For Dressler, the standards of a good material lifestyle, for example, are more than just a list of items one should own, but rather a desirable (and therefore emotional and thus motivating) measure of social identity and status. Similarly, Dressler's study of Brazilian food showed that some foods were more prestigious than others, but that specific prestigious foods varied among socioeconomic classes. The astute reader may recognize similarities in this, and the work carried out by Pierre Bourdieu described in his (1984) book, *Distinction*. Indeed, cultural models of ideal lifestyle may vary depending on group demographics—some groups may find *The Outback* restaurant fine-dining (as it is in Brazil—seriously), whereas Harvard educated New Yorkers may view it as a lowly chain restaurant. But in each, these "tastes" (in the Bourdieuian sense) are cultural models, which are reflected in specific identities (as thereby, again, emotional and motivational) (for explicit comparisons of Bourdieu and cognitive anthropology, see Strauss & Quinn, 1997).

To reiterate, what differentiates a model from a schema is scale: models are more complex and cannot be held within working memory. It is easy for most people to describe the schema for ordering food at a restaurant. It is much more difficult to articulate all the (nuanced) meanings "food" can take within Brazilian society. Because models are so complex and comprised of implicit knowledge, they cannot often be inquired about directly. Rather, a suite of methodologies (some of which are presented in this volume) are required to elicit this implicit cultural knowledge.

FINAL THOUGHTS ON PROTOTYPES, SCHEMAS, AND MODELS

To conclude this chapter, we draw readers' attention to some important aspects they might keep in mind when identifying and working with these units of cultural knowledge. First, there is a distinction between shared and idiosyncratic knowledge. So-called cultural models are shared among members of a society; but personal models operate as a function of individual biography (D'Andrade, 1995; Dressler, 2005). Personal idiosyncratic models are the product of a unique biographical history and varying experiences, while cultural models are shared among a population or community, propagated and reproduced through patterned behaviors, discourse, and public symbols. That is, cultural models are learned through social interaction and comprise tacit and explicit knowledge. Any individual's knowledge (aggregate of prototypes, schemas, and models) possesses both shared and idiosyncratic dimensions. Cognitive anthropological methods focus on the shared, and hence, cultural knowledge, but also on distinguishing that cultural knowledge from idiosyncratic personal understandings.

Second, cultural knowledge is not uniformly shared among all members of a community, nor is it immutable. No two individuals hold identical models for a given domain. The distribution of cultural knowledge is heterogeneously distributed and when combined with unique life histories, it becomes "physically impossible for any two people to hold identical cultural configurations" (Handwerker, 2002, p. 109). Importantly, no single person cognitively possesses the entirety of a cultural model, though some individuals may have more knowledge of a certain cultural model compared to other members of the community. For instance, in a fascinating series of papers, Chavez et al. document that Latinas, Anglo women, and physicians have slightly different models of breast and cervical cancer risk—in part patterned by the degree of enculturation with Western (and Anglo) biomedicine (Chavez et al., 1995, 2001). Cultural models are also subject to change because individual cognition is not static. Interactions with others can lead to new configurations of models. Emigration and immigration can cause the loss or addition of knowledge, and innovations can serve as mutations in a similar way that social memes spread rapidly through a community. Indeed, we wonder how many readers know the first step of using a rotary-phone (hint: it's not dialing the number). Technology is a prime mover of the addition and subtraction of cultural knowledge in today's world.

Third, cultural knowledge can be contextually applied and may not be in harmony with other held cultural models. Individuals participate in multiple cultures and numerous subcultures, each containing their own orthodox and heterodox models that the individual must call upon and negotiate in different circumstances. The movement from one set of cultural models to others requires cognitive and cultural negotiation to reconcile behaviors in sync with one set of models but out of sync with another (see Dengah & Thomas et al., 2019). For example, Snodgrass and his team documented the pressures of competing sets of "success" models among online video gamers (Snodgrass, Dengah, & Lacy, 2014). What constitutes success in offline settings is often both replicated and also challenged by what counts as successful *World of Warcraft* play, which also requires much time and resource investment (like in how success is achieved in widely shared American successful models) but directed towards different aims ("non-serious" play activities, which can detract from more "serious" mainstream success goals).

Finally, cognitive anthropologist Victor De Munck has asked, "Do cultural models exist in the mind or only in publications?" (De Munck, 2020). To put it another way, are cultural models "real" phenomena that exist in individual minds, which in turn are themselves culturally shared between individuals? While this may seem an overly philosophical sort of question, it does have important implications for the field and the methods we describe in this book. The cultural models we (cognitive and psychological anthropologists) seek to describe and understand are just that— models. Models are simplified representations of things, allowing the ability to perceive things that cannot be readily observed (as in the classic model of an atom found in most high school science labs). If we accept the definition of culture as learned and shared knowledge, cultural models are approximate representations of this knowledge. And it bears mentioning that the methods employed to uncover this knowledge are somewhat artificial. That is, much like trying to understand "normal" sleep behavior in a laboratory setting by having a volunteer sleep in a strange bed, hooked up to numerous machines, all while being watched via a one-way mirror, the anthropological interview and data collection techniques we describe in this book were developed to help researchers infer more complex cultural realities via somewhat artificial "elicitation" (i.e., formal interview) methods. (This is why these methods complement and enhance, not replace, traditional participant-observation, which seeks to document culture in a more natural setting.) So, while not offering a 1:1 reproduction of mental phenomena, the cultural models, schema, and other patterns of knowledge these methods elicit do explain a great deal of culturally experienced reality. And as we will see in later chapters, particularly with regards to "cultural consonance" research, these representative models can predict a wide range of behavioral and health outcomes.

In the remainder of the book, we will look at specific methodologies for eliciting cultural knowledge from informants, along with the analytical techniques to evaluate the degree of sharing and heterogeneity in relationship to particular cultural domains. The techniques we describe can be extended to more complex kinds of cultural understandings—such as theories and even worldviews—though we'll focus mostly on simpler socially learned and shared schemas and models.

3 Cultural domain analysis
Free lists

Based on what was presented in the previous chapter, one might ask: *Well, what exactly is a "cultural domain," and how do we observe it?* In many cases, such questions can feel quite daunting—culture, as many understand it, exists as a rather nebulous construct that is made up of the thoughts, behaviors, traditions, customs, and artifacts of a given group of people (according to Tylor's famous definition; Tylor, 1871; see also Kroeber & Kluckhohn, 1952). So, trying to parse out the individual components of such a thing can seem complicated. (How do you define culture when *everything* humans think, do, and possess is considered culture?) So, rather than asking, *"What does it mean to be human?"*, we can instead set out to understand the various other cultural domains that people utilize and understand in the process of being human. And, it should be noted, we don't need to tackle the largest and most complex cultural domains all at once. That is, we can instead further focus our investigation and ask how people cognitively and culturally arrange aspects of their life, such as food, behaviors, social relations, and much more. This first step is outlined in this chapter—a process called free listing.[1] As readers will learn in this chapter, free listing enables us to learn more about the constituent parts of cognitive cultural domains. Specifically, free listing helps researchers illuminate the content of individual cultural domains, while the subsequent chapter (on pile sorting) helps clarify the shape and structure to this information (Johnson, Weller, & Brewer, 2002; & Weller & Romney, 1988).

The basic process of free listing is fairly intuitive: if you want to know what people think about a certain cultural feature or set of features, you ask them to talk about it—that is, you elicit it in their speech (free listing is referred to as an "elicitation" technique, a term we explained earlier). If you want to know more about how people think as Americans, you interview and interact with them to see what characteristics, thoughts, or beliefs make up their thought. You might be thinking: *Isn't this just a standard interview? Aren't we just talking to people and learning more about them?* To a certain extent, yes—at the heart of free listing is a drive to understand respondents' perceptions of the world, much like as in a semi-structured interview. A free list, however, asks a respondent to brain-storm, or list, all the items indicative or associated with a given domain. What differentiates free listing as a method from something like developing a grocery list is that free listing establishes a formal process for understanding how items are cognitively expressed by individuals, linked to each other, and shared with other persons in a cultural domain. Free lists allow social scientists to uncover the components that contribute to an individual and collective understanding of a given cultural domain. When asking someone, *"What does it mean to be an American?"*, we are really asking them to tell us about the myriad features that conceptually create an American identity. Once replicated, with more informants and data, we can begin to see a cultural domain take shape—some items are recurrent and frequently cited, while others are more idiosyncratic, uncommon, and thus personal rather than cultural. By investigating and noting the more salient items, we clarify the content of a cultural and cognitive domain—being an American

---

[1] Careful readers will notice the various spellings of "free list" and "pile sort," sometimes presented as two words, other times as hyphenated, and occasionally as a single compound word. We follow the standard within the literature which spells these methods as two words, while reserving hyphenated versions for when the word is used as an adjective, as in "free-list data." The compound word version is used solely in reference to the software *Visual Anthropac*, which uses the "freelist" and "pilesort" in their title and interface.

means being X, Y, or Z, for instance. Free lists can thus reveal cognitively salient and mutually shared understandings of a cultural domain.

This chapter represents a first step in understanding how and what constitutes a cultural domain and how these features can be arranged cognitively. Free listing allows researchers to know more about the constituent parts of a schema or of a more full-blown cultural model. Moreover, free listing provides researchers with the skills and knowledge needed to utilize a number of other methods that we will detail in later sections of this handbook—knowing what makes up a cultural or cognitive domain can then allow you to think about both for whom the items are salient and why these features emerge and under what circumstances. To help readers think more concretely about free listing as a method, the remainder of this chapter discusses how the method has been used as a research tool (both by others in the social sciences and in our own research), and shows you how to perform this method. The latter half of this chapter will introduce readers to a common free listing software, *Visual Anthropac—Freelists* (Borgatti, 1992), provide instructions on how to import, manipulate, and analyze free-list data, and then outline how to apply these skills, via a number of exercises with an attached dataset and worksheet. Free listing is the first step towards understanding how the cultural is reflected in cognition, and by understanding this method, you can begin to apply these lessons in your own research.

FREE LISTS: ADDICTION, RACE, AND AVATARS

The use of free lists as a method for data collection and analysis can provide a researcher with the tools to understand how an informant thinks about a particular phenomenon. By looking for patterns across multiple informants, we can ascertain how members of a cultural group understand a specific domain. The development of these methods finds its roots in some of the earliest forms of social science, e.g., in early research on kinship networks (Lévi-Strauss, 1969). Social scientists have long been interested in knowing how people categorize and classify knowledge—e.g., what makes someone a member of this tribe, the different ways of saying "snow" (Regier, Carstensen, & Kemp, 2016), and the kinds of fauna and flora group members recognize and know about (Zank & Hanazaki, 2012). Most important for our discussion is how free lists can be used to understand cognitive models and thus mental formulations. *What does it mean to be an American? What feelings are associated with success or failure? How do people perceive a breach of social customs?* Through free listing, answers to these questions (and many more) can be clarified.

Let's look at some examples of research that have utilized free listing. Substance abuse and addiction are two primary areas of concern for public health workers, as they impact not just the individual, but also those individuals' larger social worlds. In developing a public health agenda to combat addiction, researchers in the United States more typically utilize a biomedical approach, but moral and emotive claims also shape addiction (Heather, 2017; Levy, 2013). And better understanding those latter dimensions of addictive processes could help public health workers better combat this form of suffering (White & Kelly, 2011). In order to parse out some of the cultural features of addiction, Henderson and Dressler performed a free list activity with undergraduate college students to see how those students perceived addiction and its causes (Henderson & Dressler, 2017). Prompting respondents to consider all possible causes or factors that might influence addition, the two recorded responses on notecards and further probed what individual terms meant and how they might be similar or dissimilar to each other. Gathering a list of 28 items, Henderson and Dressler showed that addiction etiology included aspects traditionally connected to biomedical models (e.g., genetic predispositions, the addictive properties of certain substances, and so forth). But respondents' lists also included items associated with cultural norms (such as one's social class, lacking a supportive environment, or peer pressure), as well as terms related to poor mental health (e.g., using substances for self-medication and to relieve stress, oftentimes as a coping mechanism for other mental health issues). Taken together, these results demonstrate how "addiction" as a cognitive frame is viewed as a constellation of salient features that go beyond biomedical explanations favored by public health officials. Data from studies such as this could then be utilized to explain larger, societal issues surround addiction, such as *How might collective norms and understandings about addiction and the addicted shape public policy?* or *What happens to funding and health programming if addiction is seen as a moral failure, rather than a biological or brain problem?*

To take another example, racial and ethnic minorities suffer from poorer health outcomes (we will explore more fully relationships between identity, culture, and health in Chapter 6 when we discuss cultural consonance). Being that most contemporary anthropologists now understand race to be a cultural construct, rather than a biological phenomenon, Lance Gravlee wanted to understand how racial categories were socially conceived in Puerto Rico (Gravlee, 2005). He ultimately wanted to explain why racial minorities had higher blood pressure, and he suspected that stigma might play a role. As an early step in his study, he needed to better define racial and ethnic categories from local points of view. Noting the "elasticity and ambiguity of Puerto Rican racial terms" (Duany, 2002, p. 241), previous research had indicated that more than a dozen racial distinctions were made by Puerto Ricans when discussing color, which is much more than the relatively static distinctions found in the mainland United States. Utilizing free lists over the course of 23 interviews, Gravlee generated a list of 20 racial categories used to describe Puerto Ricans, including common terms such as *blanco, trigueño, indio,* and *negro,* as well as less used ones like *rubio* and *carabalí.* Later using pile sorts and multidimensional scaling, both of which will be described in Chapter 4, Gravlee found that these racial categorizations varied based around perceptions of skin tone and hair form (Gravlee, 2005). Through this study, Gravlee argued that race was not just a sociological or anthropological construct, but also as a cognitive model in the minds of his informants.

OUR LAB: AVATAR ALTER-EGOS IN VIRTUAL WORLDS

With the continued growth and expansion of the internet, the formerly clear lines between our offline and online selves have started to blur. As part of a larger research agenda, Dengah and Snodgrass wanted to know more about how people constructed avatars in the video and computer games they played. Past ethnographic inquiries had shown that some people tended to construct an avatar that mirrored their real-life appearance, personality, and attitudes (Yee, 2014), but others tended to use virtual avatar selves as escapes from normative reality and its restrictions, with bankers (or academics) by day turning into elves by night (Bessière, Seay & Kiesler, 2007; Nardi, 2010). We wondered, *what causes someone to create an avatar that looks and behaves like themselves? And what causes someone to do just the opposite, instead creating an idealized (or even villainous) alter-ego?* Interested in better these processes, we developed a free-list protocol (Dengah & Snodgrass, 2020). Interviewing 21 gamers, we asked respondents to list traits they associated with their various selves—actual, avatar, and ideal. In their responses, interviewees sometimes listed qualities like the height, weight, gender, and race of their various selves. Others listed items such as *caring, selfless,* and *lawful,* though terms like *cruel, selfish,* and *immoral* also appeared. Other forms of analysis (described in the next chapter) will show how some these terms clustered together with each other. But straightforward free-list analyses, the focus of this chapter, showed how interviewees' avatars resembled more their actual selves when describing positive traits, but their ideal selves when detailing negative characteristics (or more precisely, how avatars, as stand-ins in some sense for ideal selves, lacked many negative characteristics respondents connected with their actual selves). We interpreted these results to suggest that when constructing avatars in virtual worlds, our videogamer respondents were inclined to reproduce positive, and minimize negative, aspects of their real-life selves.

These are but a few examples of studies that have used free listing as a method for examining the ways in which culture, as socially shared thought and practice, can be revealed through careful examination of the thoughts and beliefs of individual social actors. What follows next is an in-depth guide on how to use software for collecting and then analyzing free-list data, with illustrations from the software, *Visual Anthropac*.

SOFTWARE GUIDE: *VISUAL ANTHROPAC—FREELISTS*

Visual Anthropac is free software that enables analysis of free-list data in an easy to understand format. There is an older version of *Anthropac* that utilizes the *DOS* operating systems for computers. For those readers who were born in this century, *DOS* is an operating system developed in 1981, and is no longer natively supported by most *Windows* or *Apple* computers. There is no good reason to suffer attempting to use the original *Anthropac* for free listing. Please download the much improved *Visual Anthropac* and open the software in order to follow along with the instructions provided below (http://www.analytictech.com/anthropac/anthropac.htm). (Downloading *Anthropac* will give you access to both *Visual Anthropac—Freelists* and *Visual Anthropac—Pilesorts*, both free, with the latter featuring in the next chapter. While you're at it, you can download *UCINET 6* from the Analytic Technologies site (http://www.analytictech.com/products.htm) which we'll use for cultural consensus analysis in Chapter 5. While *UCINET* is not free (it's $40 for students), you can download a demo version for this book's exercises, and then decide if you'd like to purchase it. And a special shout out to the good folks at *Analytic Technologies*—Steve Borgatti, who developed the software, and Roberta Chase, who handles operations—their products facilitate many of the analytical routines described in this book.)

DATA COLLECTION PHASE

(1) Ask individuals to list all of the terms they can think of that are characteristic of, or representative of, a particular domain. For example, "please list all birds, symptoms of addiction, indicators of success, etc., that you can think of...."
  • Sometimes, particularly for more complex domains, informants will list more items if you give them an amount or goal to aim towards. "Try to list at least 10 things that are important to be a good Brazilian woman..."
  • Regardless of # of responses, always ask if they can think of "any more items" or "one more example."
(2) Record the items with as much fidelity as possible. We will have an opportunity to deal with synonyms during data analysis.

Note: some informants will not provide a list, but provide you with a narrative. This is okay, but will require text analysis (see Chapter 7) to yield the key terms.

(3) Sampling: This depends on the population of focus, and the domain in question. For well-established domains, sample sizes as low as 15 may be adequate, though 30 is often the standard (Handwerker, 2002; Handwerker, Hatcherson, & Herbert, 1997; Handwerker & Wozniak, 1997). Generally, you want to continue to interview respondents until the researcher hits a point of data saturation—where further interviews are no longer generating novel terms.

DATA ANALYSIS PHASE

(1) Open a text document (or any word processor program, just make sure you save your file as .txt—saving in this format removes extraneous formatting instructions that can interfere with *Visual Anthropac*'s functioning).[2]

(2) In the text file, enter the names of each informant with a "#" in front, with each term on its own subsequent line (see Table 3.1 and Figure 3.1).

(3) Open *Visual Anthropac—Freelists*. In the graphic user interface, select: File → Import → Change "Files of Type" dropdown menu to "Text Files (.txt)" → Search in the folder where you saved your file → Click on file and press → Open.

(4) The file should load and you will be presented with a number of tabs (as shown in Figure 3.2). The default tab is: I-Frequencies. This stands for "item frequencies," and is a count of each unique term in the compiled lists. The other tabs are as follows:

- Text data: simply the converted .txt data that is visible in the program.
- I-Attr.Matrix (Item Attribute Matrix): At this point, it is only an alphabetical list of terms. This will change during analysis.
- R-Attr.Matrix (Respondent Attribute Matrix): This is an alphabetical list of all your respondents.
- R-Frequencies (Respondent Frequencies): This has the list length of each respondent, also the sum total of how often their list items were listed by others, and the average frequency that any item is listed by someone else.

TABLE 3.1

Free List Items Related to "Describe an Addicted Gamer"

#Rashail
Bad Hygiene
Oily
Acne
Poor Vision
Poor Social Skills

#Sarah
Bad Hygiene
Acne
Greasy Hair
Sunken Eyes
Bad Social Skills

#Mike
Absurd Hours
Not Sleeping
Not Social Life
Socially Awkward
Online Relationships

---

[2] Also be careful of downloading as a .txt file a document that was previously stored in another format, such as a Google document, as that may inadvertently incorporate hidden formatting.

FIGURE 3.1   Data Entry for Free-List Analysis in *Visual Anthropac—Freelists.*

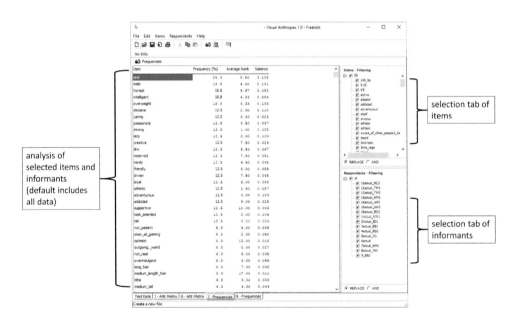

FIGURE 3.2   Imported Free-List Data Using *Visual Anthropac—Freelists.*

(5) Now comes the interpretive aspect of this analysis. You need to reduce the number of
terms via synonyms and similarity. This needs to be done with an eye towards fidelity
to the data and the domain, important emic (or cultural insider) phrasing, and an understanding of how this data will be used in later research phases. As Bernard (2017) notes,
free listing is often a prelude to other types of data collection and analysis.

Note: Combining Rules cannot be saved or easily undone. That is, all sorting rules are lost/reset when the program closes. So be sure to export all data at the end of the session.

There are two primary ways to combine terms in *Visual Anthropac*. These should be utilized in the proper order (Figure 3.3).

- Items → Recoding (Soundex) (Figure 3.4). A primary function of this tool is to combine terms with similar spellings. For example, if in a domain about emotion, you have two entries "happy" and "happy demeanor," you may want to combine them in a single "happy" term.
    - Going to items → Soundex will open a split-window with the full list of terms on the left-hand side, and suggested similar terms on the right. The term on the left will be replaced by the term on the right. Click "Apply" → "Yes." And repeat. When complete, press "OK." Pressing "Cancel" will reverse all prior changes made in Soundex.

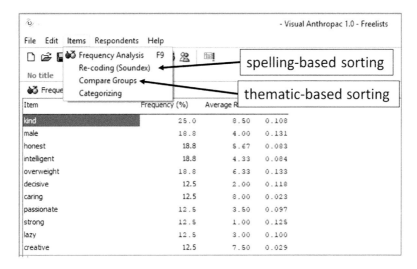

FIGURE 3.3   Categorization Tools in *Visual Anthropac—Freelists.*

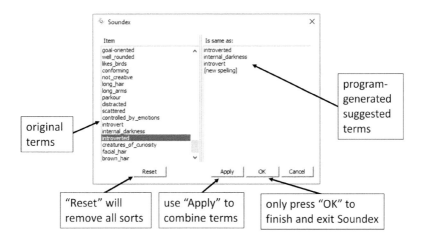

FIGURE 3.4   Soundex Sorting in *Visual Anthropac—Freelists.*

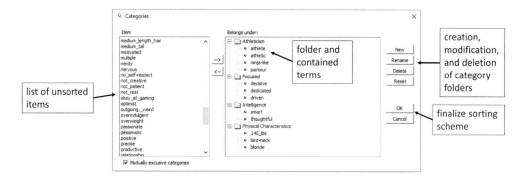

FIGURE 3.5   Thematic Sorting Categories in *Visual Anthropac—Freelists.*

  – You can also use Re-coding to group together synonyms. With a chosen term
    selected in the left-hand column, double-click "new spelling" on the right. A new
    window will allow you to enter a new spelling. After manually entering in the
    new term, click "Apply" to make the replacement.
- Items → Categorizing (Figure 3.5). The second way of reducing and combining
  terms is by creating groups. Here, you will create a hierarchy of folders (one level
  deep) to sort terms. This hierarchy categorizing will be visible in later analysis.
  Again, this will bring up a split screen window with the original terms on the left,
  and the new categories on the right. All analysis will show results at the folder and
  the item level.
  – The right window comes with a blank folder ready. Right click on the folder to
    bring up a drop-down menu. On the far right-hand side of the window, there are
    additional buttons that will allow you to create new folders, rename, delete and
    reset (which will make you lose any prior categories).
  – You can drag and drop terms back and forth to create and test out new category
    groupings. You can also press the arrow bars that are located in between the split
    windows.

*Note: You must separately "click" on the folder in the right split window BEFORE moving any
terms over. If done correctly, you will see a very faint gray bar over the folder. Otherwise, the
term will automatically be placed in the prior selected folder. Be aware, any unsorted terms will
not be included in the analysis. When terms on satisfactorily sorted, press okay.*

- You will be given a new I-Frequencies Tab, which shows analytics at the folder- and
  term-level now. The results can be read in the following metrics (see Figure 3.6):

FREQUENCY: how often term appears across informants.
AVERAGE RANK: the order in which it appears.
SALIENCY: the position of the term divided by the number of items in the list—overall saliency is the
average scores across all respondents.

*Note: You will not be able to switch to other tabs after Categorizing without re-running
Respondents-Frequency Analysis, or clearing out the categorization scheme.*

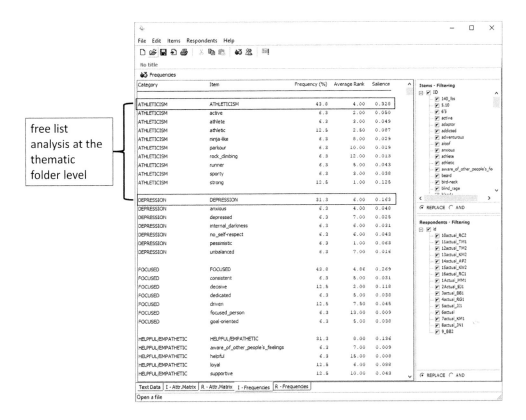

free list analysis at the thematic folder level

FIGURE 3.6 Results of Thematic Analysis in *Visual Anthropac—Freelists.*

FILTERING AND COMPARING GROUPS

- There are several ways to look at specific groups, or to only retrieve certain sets of terms. First, you can compare groups via Items → Compare Groups. This will bring up a pop-up window where you can select informants to compare. Alternatively, in the far right-hand tab, you will see two boxes, one containing all the terms and another containing all the informants. You can select or unselect terms and individuals to look for group differences. Selecting "Replace" will allow you to look at a single term of informant, whereas "And" will allow you to select multiple items or respondents. You will need to rerun the analysis for each selection (Items → Frequency analysis *OR* Respondent → Frequency Analysis).

SAVING RESULTS

- There is no way of saving progress in *Visual Anthropac*. But you can export the current analysis in .txt and excel files. File → Save All Matrices will save all current *Anthropac* tabs as .txt files, where File → Save As will save only the currently selected (opened) tab. File → Export → Excel will save the current tab as an excel file.

EXERCISE: ADDICTED GAMERS

Now that you know a little about how free lists are used in social science research and have had the opportunity to look over *Anthropac*, let's try out the software together. Please locate in this book's supplementary materials the dataset associated with this module; it is titled, "Ch3_Addicted Gamers_ Free List.txt." This is a re-creation of an elicitation exercise that we had conducted in a lab environment, where we asked 10 college students to list terms that they would use to describe what an "addicted" gamer would look like. We were interested in knowing how these terms might differ based on whether the respondent was a non-gamer, a gamer, or even a self-described "addicted" gamer. Once you have located the dataset, refer back to the software instructions provided earlier so that you can import the dataset and familiarize yourself more with the names and uses of each menu within *Visual Anthropac—Freelists*. Once you're ready, let's work together to perform a quick analysis on these free lists (see Appendix 1 for the answer key to these and all other chapter exercises):

(1) A quick and easy way to familiarize yourself with your data is with the Item-Frequencies tab (seen as I-Frequencies in *Anthropac*), which displays each item's frequency, average rank, and salience. (a) Looking at the data, which item has the highest frequency across all respondents? (b) What was this item's average rank, and (c) what does this factor mean?

(2) Before performing any analyses, it is recommended that you first attempt to refine the data by linking together similar terms, specifically those that are synonymous with one another. The Item Attribute Matrix in *Anthropac* shows all terms listed by respondents in alphabetical order. After reviewing all these terms, let's try to recode some items together, based on their similarities. (a) Find all instances that relate to the term *lonely* and recode them together using the Re-coding (Soundex) feature in *Anthropac*. Which terms did you end up selecting?

Note: This process can involve some serious deliberation—the likeness or unlikeness of terms can result in major changes to your data, so be specific and precise when determining which terms to recode and which ones to not. Much of these minute differences can be informed by ethnographic methods and work in the field—while on paper you might have two terms that appear similar, when described by your respondents, their "true" meanings could be ethnographically distinct.

(3) Once you've gone through and cleaned the data, you can also analyze data based on Respondent features. Use the Respondent frequencies tab in *Anthropac* to determine (a) who had the longest list of terms and (b) who had the highest average frequency? (c) What does it mean to have the highest average frequency, and (d) what does this mean in terms of real-life comparisons between respondents?

(4) You can also compare results from specific respondents. Let's look into how Bethany, Smeeta, and Rashaad listed terms in this free list. Use the Compare Groups menu to look into how these three listed terms they would associate with addicted gamers. (a) Viewing the item frequencies table, what was a term that all three respondents used? (b) What was a term that only Bethany and Rashaad used? (c) And what were terms that Smeeta used, but were not used by the other two?

(5) A quick and easy way to view items or data from specific respondents would be to use the filtering features on the right-hand side of *Anthropac*. These filters can be used to quickly select only certain items or respondents for analysis. Using these filters, select Arthur, Jeremy, and Max and then hit the "Run analysis, show item statistics" icon in *Anthropac*'s icons menu at the top. (a) In the updated Respondent Frequencies tab, who has the highest frequency sum out of these three, and (b) what does this feature mean pragmatically?

(6) As noted in the end of the software guide for *Anthropac*, data cannot be saved in *Anthropac* itself. Once you've finished the assessments in this chapter, be sure to save your data for future use. Save your work in this section as a .txt file that can be later imported and reevaluated in *Anthropac*.

CONCLUSION

When it comes to understanding how the cognitive and cultural features of life shape and are shaped by one another, free lists are a simple yet powerful social scientific method. As this chapter has explained, free lists enable researchers to understand the specific components of any given cultural model or domain. This is the first and elementary stage of many of the methods that are explained throughout the remaining sections of this handbook—by setting the stage and thinking more concisely about what constitutes the cultural world around us, the somewhat more advanced methods that follow will start to take form. The following chapter flows naturally from the lessons you've just learned about free lists. Now that you've gathered some of the data about what makes up a cultural model, you next need to learn about how members of a culture might cognitively organize, categorize, and give meaning to these cognitive objects. The next chapter will discuss pile sorting, a practice that takes the content that you've gathered from free lists and gives them structure and shape. By learning how to use pile sorting, researchers will begin to understand how members of a culture draw boundaries around and delineate categories within the items that constitute a cognitive-cultural domain, gaining analytical insight into the structure of culture as shared meanings and understandings.

4 Cultural domain analysis
Pile sorts

The complexities of social life can seem staggering at times, when one stops to think of the amount of information humans process daily. *How do you get dressed in the morning? Are you going to work or to school? Or maybe neither? What will you eat for breakfast?...* and that's all within an hour of waking. The human brain needs to quickly and efficiently identify, classify, interpret, and react to a barrage of sensory data, much outside of conscious awareness. The methods discussed in this chapter, again, part of what we are calling "cultural domain analysis," function to reveal some of the underlying classificatory schemes people use to think about their world.

As discussed in the previous chapter, free listing is an exploratory technique that gives researchers an understanding of the content of a cultural domain, and how that cultural knowledge might differ across individuals according to their social groups. Through interviewing and participant-observation, cognitive anthropological investigators also begin to get a sense of the sociocultural sources that shape individual group members' knowing. But in addition to understanding the content of a given domain of understanding, researchers need ways to categorize and classify the structure of that information, in ways that follow group thinking. To accomplish this, we turn to pile sorting—a natural extension of the more exploratory approach of free listing. Pile sorts allow hypothesis generation about the underlying features and structure of a cognitive domain. Specifically, the pile-sort method allows researchers to understand the similarities and differences between different items generated from free listing— *what goes with what*, so to speak. In practice, pile sorting allows researchers to identify what cultural domain items can be sorted or grouped with what other like items, and thus distinguished from items in other piles. Viewing the data in this way reveals the structure of cultural domains, including the items that are at the center as opposed to on the periphery of that domain of understanding. Additionally, this technique doesn't just show what features constitute a culturally shared domain of knowledge, but also who within a given setting understands the items in that way, allowing researchers to see individual and sub-cultural diversity lying behind what is sometimes conceived of as a monolithic Culture (with a capital "C").

It is important to note that pile sorts are more than just a task for sorting and arranging items on index cards (or perhaps digitally). It is a full-fledged interviewing technique onto itself. The piles of terms create a quantitative dataset (actually, a similarity matrix, more on that below), but also qualitative data, as the informant explains the reasoning and logic behind their sorting decisions. Taken together, pile sorts provide for both an understanding of how a cultural domain is organized, as well as the meanings behind this structure. It should be little surprise, therefore, that anthropologists have used the pile-sort technique profitably. For example, once one identifies the useful plants within a hunter-gatherer society, one can begin to ask how specifically they think about these plants and why (Liu et al., 2016; Prance, Campbell, & Nelson, 1977). *Are some plants thought of as similar due to their medicinal properties? Or, are plants typically identified according to where they're found and cultivated?* In some cases, it may be straightforward enough to just ask respondents the answers to these questions; however, the tacit and socially learned knowledge underlying cultural domains is not always consciously available to culture members. *What emotions are felt when experiencing failure? What stigmas are associated with addiction? How does gender shape language and morality?* For these questions (and many others), culture members may not themselves know why they think (and speak and behave) the way they do. Pile sorting enables researchers to see beneath the noise of everyday thought and behavior, and to potentially identify a few dimensions (cognitive organizing principles, in this case) that shape that thinking (and behaving too). Rather than forcing individuals to grapple with complex concepts in the abstract, a pile-sorting activity instead allows respondents to reveal their thinking via their sorting (grouping) of like and different items in a domain of understanding.

After providing more context and background into how pile sorting has been used by other researchers, we walk readers through the steps needed to perform their own pile-sorting exercise—both in terms of data collection and analysis. By the end of this chapter, we hope that readers will feel confident enough to perform a pile-sorting activity with a dataset that we have provided. Working through this chapter's accompanying worksheet will familiarize readers with the software we recommend—*Visual Anthropac—Pilesorts* (Borgatti, 1992) (again, download-able as part of *Anthropac* at http://www.analytictech.com/products.htm)—and help them acquire the practical knowledge needed in this form of analysis.

PILE SORTING: STIGMA AND ADDICTION

As you know by now, pile sorts allow researchers to analyze how people arrange, categorize, and classify items in a cognitive domain. Free listing is the precursor step to this method. The strength of free listing comes from that technique's ability to answer cultural domain content questions from an emic rather than an etic perspective, drawing upon respondents' own interpretations of reality. Pile sorting extends this technique, by helping researchers appreciate how culture members categorize—again, in their own (emic) terms—items within that domain of understanding. The principle behind the pile-sort analysis is relatively simple, even if the math is slightly more complicated: Successive pile sorts create a similarity matrix between each of the sorted items, which can then be graphed in two dimensions (or more) to show similarities and differences as a function of spatial coordinates (i.e., using multidimensional scaling, or MDS). (You can think of this as successive pile-sorts being overlaid onto one another.) Objects that are often grouped together are displayed closer together than dissimilar items. We will show some examples of pile-sort studies below. And don't worry about the complex math, as computer programs have all but automated the process of pile-sort analysis—but the interpretation of the results, as always, requires ethnographic insight.

Stigma is a complex psychosocial construct, which mixes emotions such as grief with social devaluation and ostracism (Link & Phelan, 2001). Pile sorting offers a novel window into these processes, as revealed by research conducted by Sayles and colleagues, in a study examining the role that stigma played in the health outcomes and lived experiences of HIV-positive men and women in Los Angeles (Sayles, Ryan, Silver, Sarkisian, & Cunningham, 2007). Building on previous work that detailed how stigma surrounding HIV impacts health-seeking behaviors and outcomes (Carr & Gramling, 2004), Sayles and her fellow researchers conducted a pile-sorting activity to determine how stigmas impacted the day-to-day livelihoods of the HIV-positive individuals in their sample. Via a series of linked focus groups, Sayles and associated generated four cognitive domains related to HIV stigma. First, stigma manifested through persistent instances of *blame and stereotyping*, where the individual was constantly reminded of their devalued status as a carrier. Second, respondents created a domain associated with *fears of contagion*, where stigma was cast by both themselves and others as anxieties regarding the spread of HIV. A third cognitive domain emerged through the stigmatizing experiences of *disclosing their status* as a carrier of HIV to friends, family, work employers, or other medical providers. Finally, HIV-positive individuals noted how their stigmatized status often resulted in them having to *renegotiate social contracts*, a taxing and stressful endeavor of finding safe and accepting environments of their medical status and the conflicts of identity that come with it.

Just through the relatively simple exercise of having respondents pile sort like terms with other like terms (related to HIV-positive status), these researchers were able to better specify the structure of thought and attribution underlying HIV stigma. They were then able to generate evidence-based claims about the social and cognitive framings of stigma, and also how to best remedy those stigmas. Sayles et al. note that these stigmas oftentimes originated in sociocultural beliefs regarding HIV, and that these beliefs (regardless of their validity) manifested in ways that impacted the identity of individuals with the disease. Over time, these stigmas could trigger prolonged psychosocial distress, as individuals were forced to contend with issues of disclosure, finding safe and acceptable places to reveal themselves as carriers, and essentially re-invent their identity in ways that reduced internally and externally generated stigmas. In presenting claims about this cognitive domain of understanding, the authors recommended ways to reduce these stigmas, including cultivating supportive networks and resources from the time of diagnosis/prognosis, and various methods promoting successful integration into family/community environments.

For this next example, recall back to the Henderson and Dressler research discussed in Chapter 3 (Henderson & Dressler, 2017), which examined the contours of addiction as seen by university students. As described earlier, the free-list activity they performed revealed items related to a cultural model of addiction. Next, their intent was to move beyond understanding which items constituted this model, to how items could be paired, linked, and combined to create a more comprehensive picture of individual and collective understanding of addiction within this group. Using an unconstrained pile-sorting activity, the researchers instructed university student to arrange the items generated from the free list into any arrangement they felt appropriate (thus, "unconstrained"), talking through how and why certain items were grouped together, as well as discussing dissimilarities between items, and the rationale for certain groupings' existence. Data were recorded and imported into the pile-sorting software *Anthropac* (which we will describe later in this chapter). Via *Anthropac*, data were first analyzed using a multi-dimensional scaling (MDS) plot, which places items that are more similar to one another closer in proximity, while items more dissimilar are plotted farther away. Next, these plots were analyzed using cluster analysis, which applies a statistical weight and measure of "goodness of fit" in order to apply boundaries around a given grouping of items, delineating clusters for clearer analysis.

In viewing these clusters, Henderson and Dressler were able to identify five main domains related to the model of addiction as defined by university students (as shown in Figure 4.1). *Biological factors* was one such domain, encompassing biological and genetic predeterminants of addiction, as well as the how the addictive properties of drugs/alcohol manifested in biological symptoms. Another major domain clustered around items relating to the use of drugs/alcohol for relieving mental/physical stressors—that is, as a means to cope with trauma, described by these researchers as *self-medicating*. The *familial* domain largely focused on social, cultural, or class-based drivers of addiction, with items such as childhood exposure, poor family life, and poverty being included. *Individual social factors* was also found to be a prominent domain, with participants including factors such as peer pressure, social drug use, and a desire for acceptance as items within this cluster. A final cluster was formed largely around the *hedonistic* use of drugs/alcohol: for pleasure, fun, curiosity, or enjoyment. In reviewing these clusters, Henderson and Dressler were able to link various features of a cognitive model into clear and conceptual groups. The five clusters that they identify closely match many of the biomedical models that are commonplace within American culture. Whether it be biological or socioeconomic determinants resulting in predispositions to addiction, or a more care-free and casual approach to drugs and alcohol common in a university setting, the use of pile sorts helped these researchers more concretely define just how college students think about addiction. The two researchers would later utilize these models to investigate how these conceptual models and other related cultural beliefs might influence how an individual attributes stigma to cases of addiction, with that process depending on whether they saw the drug use as resulting from personal choice, or from predisposed biological and other factors largely out of one's control.

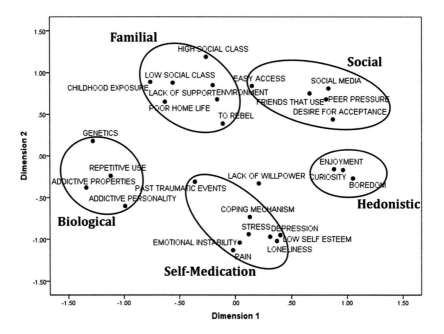

FIGURE 4.1   MDS of "Addiction" Cultural Model (Henderson & Dressler, 2017).

OUR LAB: GAMERS' EMOTIONAL EXPERIENCES
OF SUCCESS AND FAILURE

During a spring 2019 research seminar, we were interested to investigate the emotions accompanying success and failure. This was part of a larger project investigating how (video gamers') emotional responses to succeeding or failing might have lasting impacts on their mental health. As part of this investigation, we arranged a free-list activity with undergraduate and graduate students enrolled in the seminar. We first gathered terms they used to describe the feelings they had when achieving success, and then when encountering failure. Using the methods described in the previous chapter, we subsequently combined similar terms into a smaller list of items to distribute to these same individuals, who sorted the like items into piles. Again, the objective here was to see which emotion terms could be linked cognitively with one another, thinking that more salient emotion items in this domain might promote (or compromise) positive mental health.

Once data were imported and analyzed through *Anthropac* (a process described later in this chapter), we identified five "clusters" of emotions (via so-called cluster analysis) (see Figure 4.2): one that seemed to us to be related to the *pride of intellectual achievements* (feeling "right" or "smart"); another cluster of emotions pointed to more *affective responses to success* ("ecstatic," "happy," "joy," "relief"); a third revealed what seemed to be *motivational* items (with success causing respondents to feel "energized," "excited," and "motivated"); a fourth we termed *warm and fuzzy* (the two terms being "warm" and "love"); and a fifth interesting *in vivo* or "native" emotion category, the single term, *"down from here,"* which, according to the interviewee who originally listed this term, revealed the anxiety that success would invariably be followed by failure.

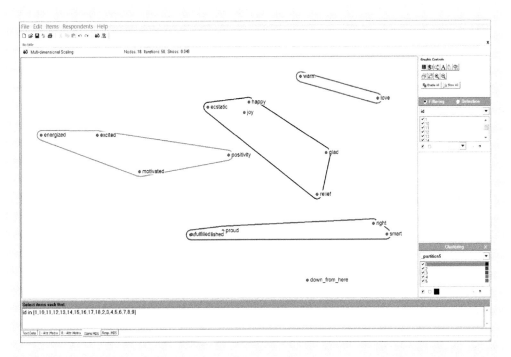

FIGURE 4.2 MDS of "Emotions of Success," Using *Visual Anthropac—Pilesorts* (Snodgrass Lab).

In addition to identifying the structure of these piles, we also performed cluster analyses on the respondents who performed the activity. There, the younger members of the respondent group and lab tended to cluster more closely together compared to the older members of our lab. In this sense, these data suggested generational differences between respondents' understandings of success, and its associated emotional states and experiences. This fairly straightforward example shows how simple it can be to understand and evaluate through software like *Anthropac* the structure of a cognitive domain—here, the domain being gamers' *emotional response to success and failure*. (For more detail on this study, see Snodgrass, Clements et al., 2020.)

Overall, whether it be culturally patterned responses to stigma, or perceptions of addiction, pile sorting enables researchers to clarify the underlying structure of cognitive domains of understanding. The following sections of this chapter will walk readers through how to perform a pile-sorting activity. As tasks and worksheets are completed, try to imagine another cultural domain you might wish to clarify, and how you would do that. Think about the items that might appear in the domain, and how they would be related to each other, and why. Think too about how you might go about eliciting the deeper structure of that domain, through the techniques described in this chapter. Thinking through questions like these will help clarify the ways in which pile sorting can be used in research.

SOFTWARE GUIDE: *VISUAL ANTHROPAC—PILESORTS* FEATURES

BACKGROUND

Pile sorting is a method for studying the relationships between items of a cultural domain, such as the items elicited from free listing. This method assesses how people cognitively think of, and order their (natural, cultural, social) world. Theoretically, this method analyzes significant overlap of these cognitive orderings across different informants and thus represents cultural (i.e., shared) knowledge (Boster & Johnson, 1989).

DATA COLLECTION MATERIALS

The instruments of this data collection method are cards (or other items), that are sorted in terms of categories of similarity and difference. The sorted items are terms elicited from other methods (including free lists or text-analysis). Each card contains one term, clearly written (for some domains, pictures may be possible, even preferable for plant/animal domains, or among samples with a high number of non-literate individuals). Each card also contains a unique number (usually on the flipside), which allows rapid recording of the contents of each pile.

METHOD: UNCONSTRAINED PILE SORT

This data collection method has no a priori constraints, or stipulations imposed by the researcher. The purpose is to elicit native categories, and groupings of the domain. Let the informants decide the important criteria for sorting items!

(1) Participants are given a set of cards and asked to look through them to familiarize themselves with the terms/items.
(2) Participants are then asked to divide the items into groups (placing similar items together).
   • The only rules are that informants can't make just a single pile and that they can't place each and every item in their own solitary pile. (The reason for this is that analysis depends on identifying cards as similar or different to each other.)
   • Encourage the participant to talk out loud through their thought processes (but do not interrupt or interfere, just record/take notes). Indeed, a pile-sort interview can be viewed as two interviews in one—the data collected from the pile sorts, but also respondents' unstructured verbalization of their thought-processes during and after the task.
(3) After completion, ask the informant to explain the sorting criteria and meaning(s) of each pile.
(4) Researchers record the items in each pile (using the unique numbers on the back of each card, as well as the criteria/meaning).

METHOD: CONSTRAINED PILE-SORT

The method is identical to that described above, except for one important difference. Rather than allowing the informant to decide the number and composition of the sorts, the research stipulates X number of piles determined by Y criteria. This allows for hypothesis testing—that there is some shared order of terms, a priori identified by the researcher. For example, you may want to have respondents sort a list of character traits by how those traits are perceived to be associated with a particular gender (that is, the researcher hypothesizes that there is culturally patterned distinction of terms, organized by gender). Or you may suspect that some indicators of the "ideal religious lifestyle" are more important than others. So, you can stipulate that informants create three piles—grouping together the terms they perceive to be *most important*, *important*, and *least important* to an ideal religious life (see Dengah, 2014).

DATA ANALYSIS: *VISUAL ANTHROPAC—PILESORTS*

BACKGROUND

This analysis creates an aggregate matrix of true/false statements (e.g., does term X belong in the same pile as term Z?) between items across informants, which will allow you to perform a variety of statistical analyses:

- Multi-Dimensional Scaling (MDS): Visual representation of similarities from pile-sort data, and shared clusters of terms
- PROFIT (Property Fitting Analysis): Dimensions by which the MDS are arranged
- Cultural Consensus: Similarities between piles sorts across informants.

HOW TO ENTER DATA

(1) Create a text document (again, ending in ".txt"). In order for the program to run properly you need to begin the file with a header (see Figure 4.3):

- DL (data language)
- nm= (this is the # of informants)

FIGURE 4.3 Pile-Sort Data Entry Using *Visual Anthropac—Pilesorts*.

- n= (this is the number of items sorted)
- format= ps
- matrix labels: labeling informants (not necessary) Single word or set of numbers, separate each with a ",". Put these in order by which your informants' data is entered.
- Labels: item labels (not necessary) Single word or set of numbers, separate each with a ",". Put these in order by the number assigned to items. Item number "1" should be the first label listed, followed by 2, etc.
- data:
  - Begin each new informant with a "#"
  - Row for each pile, separate items with ","
  - End each sort with a ";"

(2) Save the document as a .txt file.

IMPORT DATA INTO *VISUAL ANTHROPAC*

(1) Open *Visual Anthropac—Pilesorts*
(2) File → Import → (change drop down menu to search for .txt file) → (find file) press Open
       You will receive an initial MDS in the "Items MDS" tab (Figure 4.4). Other tabs include:

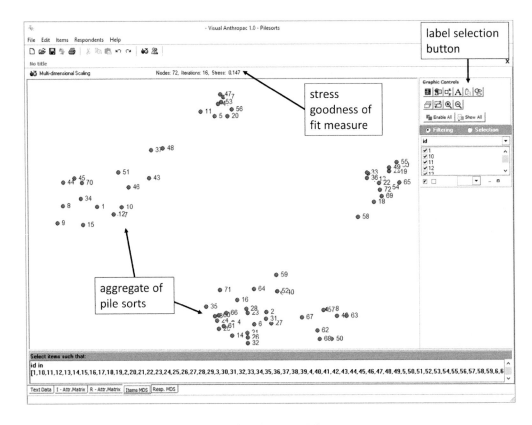

FIGURE 4.4   Pile-Sort Analysis Using *Visual Anthropac—Pilesorts*.

- Text Data: Imported raw data
- I-Attr.Matrix: Associated item labels, if included
- R-Attr.Matrix: Associated respondent labels, if included
- Resp. MDS: MDS of informant similarity

The Item MDS tab will be the primary tab for data analysis in this methodological approach. On the top border of the item MDS includes Node: ##; Iterations: ##; and Stress: 0.XXX. These are interpreted in the following ways:

- Nodes: Number of items in MDS
- Iterations: Number of MDS permutations that the program ran to arrive at this current arrangement
- Stress: A measure of MDS "fit." MDS takes multi-dimensional cultural ideas, and displays it in two dimensions. Fit is a measure of how well the data is represented in this form. Sturrock and Rocha provide levels of significance for MDS with various numbers of nodes (Sturrock & Rocha, 2000). Stress values closer to 0 will indicate that the displayed MDS fits the data well.

ANALYSIS

Assign labels to items (if included): On the right-hand side is a small panel called "Graphic Controls." Select the button with a picture of a tag with a lower-case light blue "a." This will open a window. Select the drop-down menu to select "label." Click OK. This should now apply labels to all the items.

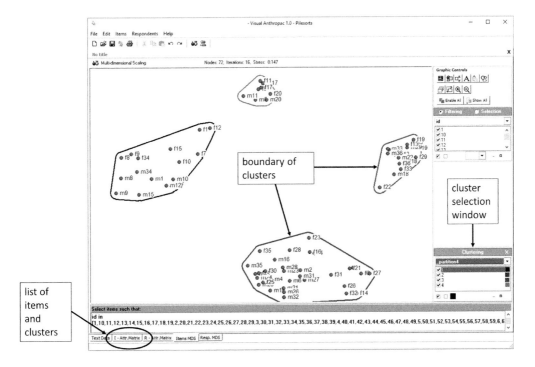

FIGURE 4.5 Cluster Analysis Using *Visual Anthropac—Pilesorts*.

CLUSTER ANALYSIS

Determine if there are statistical meaningful groupings in the MDS (Figure 4.5). This analysis requires a degree of interpretation, guided by ethnographic data. The minimal cluster number is 1, where all items are included, and the maximum number is equal to the number of nodes, with each item in its own cluster.

(1) Select, Item → Cluster Analysis → Choose Clustering method → Choose number of clusters to show (remember that the maximum number of clusters).

- Clustering methods include the following:
- Complete Link: farthest neighbor clustering.
- Single Link: nearest neighbor clustering.
- Average Link: average distance clustering (recommended).
- The number of clusters depends on ethnographic insights. For most domains, less than 10 is a sufficient starting place. Press OK.

The first cluster analysis shows a single cluster. A new window will open up in the lower right-hand side of the screen. There is a drop-down window that says "_partition 1." The drop-down menu will show different numbers of clusters.

You can also access the specific item-cluster information via the I-Attr.Matrix tab. (Note, because MDS represents multi-dimensional domains in two dimensions, sometimes there will be an "overlap" of clusters. This tab will allow you to verify which node belongs in which cluster.)

OTHER MDS OPTIONS

By first left-clicking on a node (directly on the MDS diagram), so that a black square outline is shown at the selected node, and then right-clicking on the square, an option menu, where you can change the color, size, and shape of the node. This is helpful for visual displaying items by other, a priori, known attributes. (These same options are available via the graphics controls.) You can also hold the left mouse key and drag to select a larger subset.

Through this options menu, you can also disable specific nodes. By doing this, and then switching between tabs, will rerun the MDS, but without the selected items. This can also be done with informants. This is particularly useful for looking at the MDS of certain informants by demographic data, or how a certain subset of items is sorted.

CULTURAL CONSENSUS ANALYSIS

The other primary analysis available in *Visual Anthropac—Pilesorts* is consensus analysis (see Figure 4.6).

- Respondents → Consensus. This will open a new tab that says "R-Comp.Matrix"

Cultural consensus can be viewed as a "goodness of fit" measure (i.e., how well our analytical model fits the data) for pile sorts. That is, cultural consensus tests if informants are creating piles significantly similar to one another. If consensus is reached (see Chapter 5 for more information), then there is support for that the MDS represents "shared knowledge." Each informant will be given a competency score, which represents how much their responses match those of the group (higher values indicate more similarity). In the top margin, the first eigenvalue and eigenvalue ratio are provided. These values indicate the amount of variance explained by the first and second factors. A 3:1 ratio or greater indicates "consensus." (Again, see Chapter 5 for more information about Cultural Consensus Analysis, the focus of that chapter.)

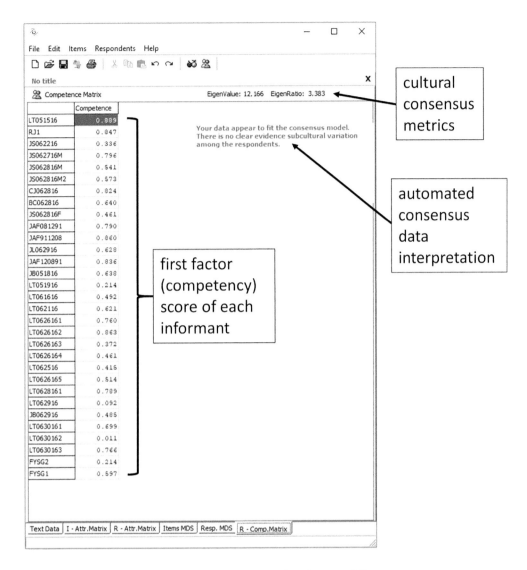

FIGURE 4.6 Cultural Consensus Analysis Using *Visual Anthropac—Pilesorts.*

Note: MDS can be done with any pile-sort technique. Though in general, it is most informative for unconstrained piles sorts.

PROFIT ANALYSIS

There is an advanced technique for analyzing the distribution pattern of items generated in the MDS diagram. That is, why are some clusters next to one another, whereas others are on the opposite side of the diagram? This procedure, known as Property Fitting (PROFIT) analysis, is a hypothesis testing procedure that examines if the dimensions of the MDS (that is, the spatial distribution of items and clusters) are patterned by a particular category or attribute. Readers should refer to Appendix 2 for complete details for how to perform this hypothesis testing technique.

EXERCISE: EMOTIONS OF SUCCESS AND FAILURE

Now that you have learned about what pile sorts are and some of the background theory behind the method, it is time for you to practice with some examples. For this activity, you will perform analyses on a mock dataset that we have generated looking at emotions experienced when respondents succeeded in difficult circumstances. After generating and iteratively developing the listed items through free-list activities, we presented these terms to respondents in a pile-sort activity. Specifically, we prompted respondents to link items in an unconstrained pile-sorting interview, allowing them to create groups as they saw fit, and only offering additional prompting when they struggled to understand what terms meant. Once completed, we noted these piles and created a text file that described the piles. You can find this dataset in the supplementary materials for this handbook (entitled, "Ch4_Emotions and Success.txt") and work through the following assignments to practice the pile-sort technique using *Anthropac*. (Again, see Appendix 1 for the answer key to these and all the book's exercises.)

First, let's import the dataset into *Visual Anthopac—Pilesorts* and examine the data:

(1) Looking at the Text Data panel is a good way to get a bird's eye view of the dataset. It shows the respondent ID, alongside the total number of piles they've created and the numbered labels associated with each term. (a) Looking at this panel and these data, are there any trends that you can immediately see? (b) What numbers/terms seem to be clustered with others (c) or are isolated? Trying to first identify these patterns can give you greater insight into future trends once you perform formal cluster analyses on the data.

(2) Now that you have a decent idea of the data that you have just imported, look at the Item MDS panel. (a) Do the items you identified as grouped together in the Text Data panel appear together in the spatial Items MDS representation of the data? (b) Or, are you seeing some new trends emerge?

(3) Now, you are going to want to give these nodes some greater clarity. In the same Items MDS panel, find the Labels icon under the Graphic Controls window on the right-hand side and give each of these nodes their correct labels (by choosing "label" rather than "id" in the dropdown menu that appears when you click that icon). Now that you have them properly named and can see some how they're arranged on the page, (a) What do you see?

(4) With everything now labeled and ready to go, it is time to do cluster analyses, starting with the items in the Items MDS panel. Using the Items menu at the top of *Anthropac*, perform your first Cluster Analysis on the emotion items (using that menu command), choosing "Average link" from the Clustering method dropdown menu that appears (this setting is recommended for your first analysis, as it's often straightforward to spot trends in this setting). For "Max clusters to show," play around with this setting a bit. It's initially set to five, but it could go up to as many as ten iterations. Select option and hit "OK" to begin your analysis. Now, using the Clustering panel in the bottom right, open up and view some Partition settings (e.g., _partition1, _partition2, etc.) to see how different clusters emerge. Look at the dataset at five partitions (_partition5): (a) What are some trends that you see in this representation of the data? (b) What items are linked together with the term *ecstatic*? (c) And what might be causing these terms to be linked together?

(5) Now that you're viewing the dataset at five partitions, you can also change the node shape and color to make future analyses more obvious. Going back to the Graphic Controls window, use the Color and Shape icons to change the appearance of the nodes the clustering it set at five partitions.

(6) Once you've done this, when you swap back to other partition settings you can see how the clustering strengths vary based on the setting. Look at the clustering found in the

partitioning set at two for example: (a) What are some obvious differences between the terms linked together when clustering is set at two compared to five partitions? (b) How might these differences in clustering be explained?

(7) One other important metric to note when discussing MDS and clustering analyses in *Anthopac* is the notion of *stress*. Here, stress refers to the goodness of fit of the items in relation to the general trend of the models presented. Look above the clusters in the main window of *Anthropac*: (a) What is the stress of this model? (b) What does this stress metric mean for this spatial representation of the pile-sort data?

(8) Many of the techniques to look at the clustering of terms can also be applied to the clustering of respondents as well. Before we get into the process of how to do that, think about these questions first: (a) Why might we be interested in knowing about the clustering of respondents in addition to items? (b) What are some reasons that might explain how people are clustered together? (c) Or reasons why they are isolated from other respondents? (d) What are some research implications for looking into the clustering of respondents in this manner?

(9) After you have thought about or discussed these ideas, it's fairly straightforward to perform cluster analyses on respondents. Navigate to the Resp. MDS panel (at the bottom of the screen). Then, using the same outlined steps as above with items, perform a cluster analysis on respondents by selecting Cluster Analysis under the Respondents tab in the top menu and answer the following when using Partition 5: (a) What cluster is the largest in the partition? (b) Who is in this group?

(10) Ethnographic and demographic information can assist in understanding how respondents could be isolated or clustered together. Based on that, (a) hypothesize why Ivan, Mika, and Clarence might be isolated from the larger group, and (b) why Rigoberta and Cathy appear together.

(11) Another key feature of Respondent analysis is the R-Agreem.Matrix, which shows how much agreement there is on a respondent-to-respondent basis (i.e., how much one respondent's piles resembled another's). The Agreement Matrix can be activated under the Respondents tab at the top of *Anthropac*, and then selecting the View/ Agreement Matrix subcategory (which will put you in the R-Agreem.Matrix panel). Once the R-Agreem.Matrix panel is opened, here are some questions to consider: (a) Which respondents have the closest agreements when it came to their pile-sorting? (A quick way to get a sense of this would be to look back at the respondent cluster analyses and see which respondents are closest to one another.) (b) What are some hypothetical reasons for why these respondents agree with each other in a particularly strong manner? Now look at the two most distant respondents: (c) Who are they? (d) What is the agreement matrix coefficient for these two respondents? (e) What might you interpret this coefficient to mean?

(12) Further, you can also view the cultural consensus scores associated with this pile-sort analysis. Recall that cultural consensus analysis can also be thought of as providing a "goodness of fit" measure for the data. Find this option under the Respondents tab (at the top of *Anthropac*, and then clicking Respondents/Consensus, which will take you to the R-Comp.Matrix panel): (a) What was the result of this consensus analysis according to *Anthropac*? (b) Are respondents similar in the way they're sorting the emotion data?

(13) Finally, now that you've analyzed the data, seen the cluster analyses, and looked into how respondents are more or less similar to one another, think more about the kinds of statements you can make based on respondents' pile-sorting activity. (a) What sorts of conclusions can be drawn from this dataset?

CONCLUSION

When attempting to describe something as complex as culture, even analyzing a single domain of shared knowledge can appear daunting. But the tools and methods described in this and the previous chapter point to the utility of a cognitive anthropological approach. Though not always explicitly theorized as such, each frame of meaning elicited through free listing and pile sorting can be understood as a socially transmitted and partially shared "cultural model" of a kind. Free listing enables researchers to parse the items composing the model (i.e., identify the model's content), while pile sorting helps researchers see the important relationship between those items (the model's structure). The next chapter helps us better understand patterns of consensus—and dissensus—in how these models are understood across individuals in a group.

5 Cultural consensus analysis

As stated earlier, one main goal of cognitive anthropology is to understand culture from an emic "cultural insider" point of view (Borgatti, 1994). And culture, from this perspective, has been famously operationalized by Ward Goodenough (1957, p. 167) as "whatever it is one must know in order to behave appropriately in any of the roles assumed by any member of a society." In essence, culture can be described as the knowledge that allows group members to operate in social situations and predict, interpret, and understand the actions, behaviors, thoughts, goals, and values of social others (Kronenfeld, 2011). Cognitive anthropological research, therefore, focuses on the ways in which shared cultural knowledge is constructed, organized, and distributed among members.

In Chapter 2, we discussed how culture can be conceptualized through the lens of what have been called prototypes, schemas, and models—mental short-hands and cognitive structures that enable individuals to make sense of an ever-changing world. Then, in Chapters 3 and 4, we examined means of constructing interview protocols and collecting data through free lists and pile sorts, which provides a grounded way to identify socially shared knowledge in what would otherwise be a more amorphous "culture." But an essential aspect of culture is that it is both shared and meaningfully distributed in a community. *How then can we test if a prototype, schema, or model is more than just an individual conceptualization, and instead reflects more generally shared group understandings? Or, as we discussed last chapter, how do we know if our informants are creating pile sorts in a non-arbitrary way?* Cultural consensus analysis (CCA), the topic of this chapter, allows us to do exactly this: to rigorously test (rather than simply presume) that a set of understandings are meaningfully shared and distributed among members of a group.

Cultural consensus analysis, developed by Romney, Weller, and Batchelder (1986), does more than estimate group responses based off of simple group means (averages) or modes (majority responses). Instead, CCA, via factor analysis, looks at culture at both the individual and aggregate level by comparing the amount of agreement between individuals (via an informant-by-informant matrix). The degree to which an individual's responses are similar or dissimilar to the entire group produces a "competency" score (ranging typically from 0 to 1), and can be generally interpreted as the percent of responses to which an informant gave a culturally accurate response. That is, if an informant has a competency score of 0.5, they may be viewed of getting 50% of the responses "correct." (Note that negative scores are possible from the formal model accounting for guessing (discussed below) and other factors.) If most informants' responses are similar to that of everyone else's, we can confidently conclude that there is shared knowledge. And if we weight each informant's replies by their competency score, we can estimate the most culturally agreed upon answers to the interview questions—or what we call a "cultural model answer key." The general rule of thumb is that consensus is found if the eigenvalue ratio of the first to second factor is greater than 3:1. (An eigenvalue is simply the amount of variance explained by a particular factor, and often these are standardized so that the total amount of variance is equal to the total number of variables. So that an eigenvalue of 10 would explain the amount of variance equal to 10 variables or informants.) Additional rules of thumb are that cultural consensus would produce average competency scores above 0.5, and that there are few to no negative competency scores. In plain English: consensus is found if most of the aggregate data can be explained by a single factor; if the aggregate of individuals responds to at least 50% of the questions culturally correctly; and no individual completely responds contrary to the group.

We can better grasp the logic behind cultural consensus via a simple example, which was used by Romney et al. in the original 1986 paper to illustrate the technique. You are in an Introduction to Cultural Anthropology course, and your professor gives you a multiple-choice midterm exam. Somehow, your professor has lost the answer key, and instead of creating a new answer key herself, she decided to use CCA to have the students reproduce the answer key. Assuming that all the questions were well written and fair, and that she did a good job teaching the material, we can assume that (1) The majority (mode) responses will often, but not always, have the correct answer. (There may be some difficult questions that only a few A and B students will get correct) and (2) Students whose answers are most like the group (these are your A and B students) will have the correct answers most often. So, the professor could use CCA to essentially see if everyone acquired the same shared information (hopefully!) and then estimate the answer key from the compiled answers. In anthropological contexts, we are doing the same thing: we are trying to estimate an answer key for the shared knowledge of a group, where no answer key was provided.

ASSUMPTIONS AND REQUIREMENTS OF CCA

There are a couple essential conditions in order to perform CCA effectively. First, informants need to respond to questions independently and separately from all other informants. It is difficult to test shared knowledge if you allow your informants to collaborate on their responses. This means that CCA is not appropriate for focus groups and similar interviews. Second, the questions need to be centered around a single cultural model and have the same level of difficulty—that is the questions should be at the same level of "cultural expertise." We would note that traditionally, a third condition states that there should only be one answer key (Weller, 2007). This condition, however, has been relaxed in light of new methodologies that look for subcultural variation and even competing cultural models (two or more answer keys) (e.g., Lacy, Snodgrass, Meyer, Dengah, & Benedict, 2018). (These advanced methods are described in Appendix 3.)

TYPES OF DATA AND SAMPLE FOR CCA

CCA can be used with multiple choice, true/false, ordinal, and rank-order data. However, the statistical analysis of the method may differ depending on the type of data. Multiple choice and true/false data can use the formal cultural consensus model, which adjusts for informant guessing. That is, if an informant doesn't know the shared response, then she will guess at the answer. Simply by guessing, she will be "correct" (i.e., concordant with the culturally shared group response) some percentage of the time, even though she does not actually share this cultural knowledge. As such, guessing may artificially inflate the perceived consensus of knowledge—and this model corrects for this. The informal model, on the other hand, does not adjust for guessing, and is most commonly used for ordinal, interval, and rank-order data. In most real-world cases, the results of both models are very similar. And in practical terms, the analysis is performed in exactly the same way in computer programs that run cultural consensus analysis.

Finally, there are some rules of thumb regarding the number of questions, the number of informants, and the like. Hypothetically, cultural consensus can be run on any number of items with any number of people. In general, at least 20 items are recommended in order to get a more fully understanding of how a model is shared (Weller, 2007). Similarly, at least

15 people are necessary to identify a widely shared (high competency across informants) model (Handwerker & Wozniak, 1997). For models that have more varied distribution of knowledge, more informants may be necessary. For example, Weller (2007) estimates that a model that has an average competency of 0.5 would require a sample size of at least 23 to be significant at the 0.01 level.

CULTURAL CONSENSUS: THE GOOD LIFE AND GOOD HEALTH

Working within this paradigm of cultural models, consensus can be seen through the works of many scholars, most notably that of Bill Dressler, who has used the technique to good effect in Brazil (Dressler, 1996; Dressler, Balieiro, & Dos Santos, 1997, 1999; Dressler, Balieiro, Ribeiro, & Santos 2009; Dressler, Dengah, Balieiro, & Santos, 2013). In work now spanning over three decades (Dressler, 2017), Dressler has widely utilized the method of cultural consensus to uncover what it means to have "a good life" in Brazilian *barrios* (neighborhoods). By investigating this central question, Dressler and his colleagues sought out what qualities, possessions, or personalities made up this cultural model of wellness in Brazil. To do so, they utilized a number of methods discussed in earlier chapters of this handbook—prolonged ethnographic fieldwork in the cultural setting, semi-formal interviews to generate free-list data, pile-sorting activities to categorize and link these terms to one another, and more. Moving from data-collection techniques to data analysis, Dressler and his team then analyzed these data using (the *DOS* version of) *Anthropac*. Once completed, Dressler was able to then create a cultural consensus model detailing the various features that would constitute a "good life" for Brazilians. These items included many basic necessities—such as showers, refrigerators, and beds—but also some more mundane items that potentially denoted class differences, like the ability to travel (both domestically and abroad), new technologies, and air conditioning. As we will discuss in the next chapter, the key linkage between health outcomes and cognitive conceptions of culture found through cultural consensus is through the use of "cultural consonance," the degree to which individuals behaviorally embody these notions of culture.

Just as Dressler and his colleagues aimed to understand more about what makes up the "good life," research from Smith et al. looked into what constituted a "good clinical experience," noting that intercultural differences between health practitioners and patients can result in varying health outcomes (Smith et al. 2004). The researchers developed free-list data from prolonged ethnographic fieldwork in hospital clinics and presented a series of relevant clinical features to patients, hospital faculty, and medical residents to determine if consensus was achieved for "a good clinical experience." In their cultural consensus analyses, Smith et al. found that there was not consensus between the three groups, indicating that each group had different cultural norms and expectations of a clinical experience. Patients, for instance, highly valued the ability to have a prolonged relationship with the same doctor, while faculty and residents place very little emphasis on this relationship ability. Conversely, findings from this cultural consensus analysis found that faculty and residents viewed the use of computers in the clinic as important sources of information and patient records, while the patients themselves found their use cumbersome and insufficient to the actual patient-doctor relationship they craved. These features, amongst many other differences between these groups, highlighted how clinical spaces often incorporate different cultural values and norms into their experiences. Here, the cultural roles that are shaped by the clinical experience can be further outlined through these cognitive models—the role and cultural norms of the patient in these analyses are shown to be distinct from the role and norms of the clinician. In presenting these data, Smith and his associates put forward a series of recommendations for the clinical experience that would resolve some of these cultural incongruities and lead to a greater clinical experience for both patient and provider (namely spending more time during clinical experiences to hear patient concerns and insights into their health).

OUR LAB: +/– GAMING EXPERIENCES AS AN ALTERNATIVE TO "GAMING DISORDER"

Drawing on the tradition of Weller, Romney, Dressler, and others, we utilized a cultural consensus framework in our own research on so-called gaming "addiction" (Snodgrass, Dengah et al., 2017). Research on the diagnostic criteria used to assess "addictive" or "disordered" gaming carries with it a fair degree of controversy, with some researchers questioning the validity the criteria for making such assessments (Aarseth et al., 2016; Griffiths et al., 2016; Saunders et al., 2017). As such, we aimed to develop a different set of criteria, driven by the long-standing ethnographic work we've conducted over the years with online gamers. Rather than assuming that problem gaming follows the same patterns seen in substance use or gambling addictions, we adopted a framework that prioritized gaming-specific positive and negative experiences, based on our long-term ethnography. Once the items were developed (from textual analysis of interviews using the software *MAXQDA*, techniques we'll discuss in Chapter 7), we performed cultural consensus analysis by having gamers rate each item's importance in an online survey (see Table 5.1).

When analyzing these data, two clear contrasts became apparent. First and foremost, when discussing and relaying the positives about gaming, there was high cultural consensus. All but one of our positive items had high consensus, indicating that when it comes to understanding the cognitive and cultural constructs of positive gaming experiences,

TABLE 5.1

Positive and Negative Gaming Experiences, Validated via Cultural Consensus

Positive Gaming Experience	Negative Gaming Experience
Positive Anticipation	Negative Cognitive Salience
Mood Improvement	Mood Deterioration
Life Focus and Purpose	Regret
Adrenaline and Energy Rushes	Draining
Positive Testing of Limits	Push Selves Too Far
Calm and Controlled	Withdrawal
Positive Routine	Bad Habit/Play Despite Problems
Testing Limits	Loss of Control/Relapse
Enjoyable Repetition	Boring Routine
Preferred Hobby	Loss of Interest in Other Activities
Positive Distraction	Avoidance/Mood Modification
Growth and Evolution	Tolerance
Social Connection	Social Isolation
Expanded POV	Need for Social Approval
Social Belonging	Toxic Community
Positive Anonymity	Negative Anonymity
Strengthened Relationships	Conflict
Positive Social Obligation	Negative Social Obligation
Satisfying Labor	Draining Job
Increased Confidence	Loss of Confidence
Career and Life Advancement	Perceived Failure

there was general agreement within our sample. Conversely, our respondents had high amounts of disagreement and conflict when considering our negative items, with only 6 of the 21 items finding high degrees of consensus. What might these results mean—both for our new psychiatric inventory and beyond? The positive items confirmed what we learned ethnographically—that the positives of gaming are apparent, observable, and well-established in the gamer community. According to our research, feelings related to success and a sense of accomplishment are some of the positive consequences of playing video games in a highly involved manner, though such emotional experiences don't typically feature in psychiatric inventories. Alternatively, the high levels of disagreement in regard to the negative terms shows that gamers themselves aren't sold on many of the pitfalls of gaming—there isn't a singular, unified notion of what it means to be "addicted" to a video-game, at least not from gamer points of view.

SOFTWARE GUIDE: *UCINET*

How to create a cultural consensus interview

Bill Dressler refers to writing the cultural consensus interview as an "art." Here, the researcher is trying to take an abstract cultural domain and condense it to a more manageable "model" or concise "frame of meaning." (And it is worth noting that a cultural model is exactly that—a conceptual abstraction or schematic model that represents or approximates something in the world.) So, the goal here is to take the important units of knowledge ascertained in earlier research phases and test their distribution among the members of a community.

Consensus can be done with dichotomous (true/false), multiple choice, Likert, and rank-order data. The optimal format depends on the cultural domain in question. In Dressler and colleagues' 1998 study of the ideal Brazilian material lifestyle (Dressler, Balieiro & Dos Santos, 1998), they simply asked if certain household goods were important or not for "the good life." A similar methodology was used by Dengah and his students (2016) to look at religious and secular gender roles. In this study, informants performed a constrained pile sort to identify which characteristics were important to a specific gender identity. This functionally resulted in a "true/false" response, with the included cards being "true" and those sorted out as "false." Likert responses, on the other hand, are ideal for allowing respondents to provide a gradient of (dis)agreement. Snodgrass and colleagues (2017) used this approach in the construction of gamer addiction models, described in the vignette above. Finally, rank orders are useful for eliciting the relative importance of some items of the domain to others. This approach was utilized by Dengah (2013) in his study of the ideal Pentecostal lifestyle. Because of the domain—the good religious life—informants would respond with "true" and "highly agree" for every item—obscuring any variation in agreement. (Remember, cultural consensus analysis is about patterns of both agreement and disagreement.) So instead, Dengah had informants perform a constrained pile-sort of 39 terms indicative of the ideal Pentecostal lifestyle. Informants created three equal piles: items that are essential; items that are important; and items that are less important. Then, he asked informants to internally rank the items in each pile from 1 to 13. Compiled, it provided the entire 1–39 set of items ranked for cultural consensus analysis.

UCINET

Data entry and analysis will be completed in *UCINET* (see Figure 5.1). Remember a few important points about this software:

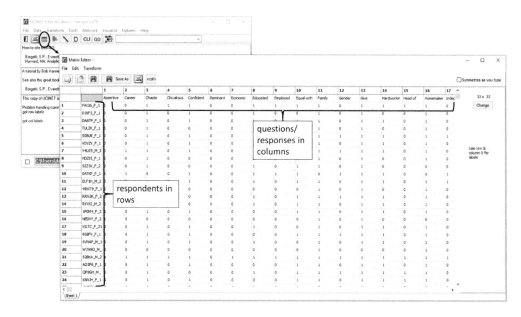

FIGURE 5.1   Data Entry for Cultural Consensus Analysis Using *UCINET*.

(1) *UCINET* will download some outputs to a default folder. At the start of each session, be sure to change the location to the desired folder. Open *UCINET* → File → Change Default Folder.

(2) Most *UCINET* analyses result in a pop-up text file displaying particular results. These are not automatically saved. Be sure to save this .txt file at the end of each analysis manually.

(3) *UCINET* is updated frequently, which usually corrects issues, but sometimes introduces new errors. If you experience this, download an older (or newer) version of this program (https://sites.google.com/site/ucinetsoftware/versions).

Data entry

Create a spreadsheet with a row of data for each informant. Have data variables numerically coded. This can also be done within the *UCINET* program itself or in another program such as *Excel*. Either option will involve entering the data directly or copying existing data into either the *Excel* Matrix Editor or the Matrix Editor (found in the *UCINET* toolbar). Save as a *UCINET* file type.

Perform consensus analysis

(1) Tools → consensus analysis

In the dialogue box, select the input dataset as the *UCINET* matrix saved in the previous step. Ensure that the Output Competencies, Output Agreement Matrix, and the Output Answer Key are all directed to the proper folder, via the ellipses (Figure 5.2). You may also want to rename these output files, as any subsequent analysis will automatically write over the previous data.

In Type of Data selection, select the type of data matrix being imported. For most datasets, the default "Profiles: A row of data for each respondent" will be selected.

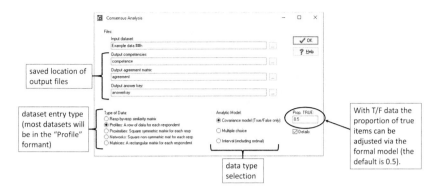

FIGURE 5.2 Analysis Options for Cultural Consensus Analysis Using *UCINET.*

For Analytical Model, select the type of data you have for each informant: true/false, multiple choice, or interval/ordinal data. For true/false, you have the option of modifying the proportion of true or false items. For most consensus analysis, leave this at 0.5. Make sure the Details box is checked. Click OK.

A new text document will appear (like shown in Figure 5.3). First, save the displayed text document (automatically labeled *UCINET*log#), as this document is not automatically saved. Go to "save as" navigate to the desired folder, rename, and save.

The first few lines provide a summary of the input parameters and the location of four automatically produced text file output documents. All of these are redundant to the current output text file, EXCEPT the second factor loading output. You will want this for any visualization of informant agreement, or for residual agreement analysis.

The next entry in this document is the informant agreement matrix, where values show the correlation between informant's responses. In general, scores range from absolute disagreement (−1) to absolute agreement (1).

The next set of data relays the results of the consensus analysis:

- No. of negative competencies: Number of individuals who have negative scores on the first factor. In other words, a negative score means that a significant amount of variation was not accounted for by the first factor.
- Largest eigenvalue: The amount of variance accounted for by a single factor.
- Second largest eigenvalue: The amount of variance accounted for by the second factor.
- Ratio of largest to next: Ratio of variance explained by the first to second factor. As a rule of thumb, this should be 3 or above, which would indicate at least some degree of consensus.
- Automated analysis of consensus: This is a canned response of whether consensus is found via traditional rules of thumb. In general, consensus is found if the eigenvalue ratio is above 3 and there are few to no negative competency scores. Additionally, the average competency (first factor) scores should be above 0.5.

Following this will be a load-out of each individual's' competence scores. These are equal to their first factor scores. Again, possible values range from −1 to 1.

After this will be raw response frequencies.

And finally, this document will contain the Answer Key. The answer key is created via weighted averages, taking an informants' competency into account. An individual whose responses are

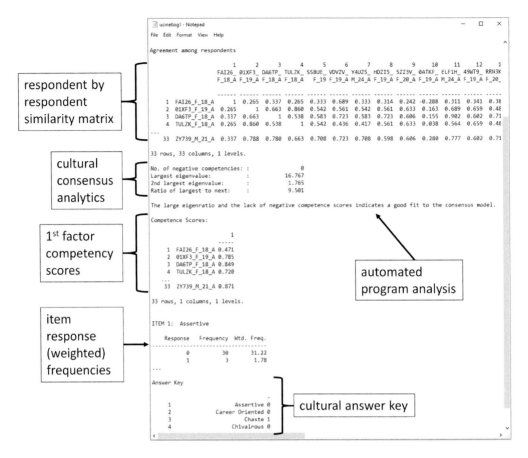

FIGURE 5.3   Cultural Consensus Output Using *UCINET.*

more similar to the aggregate will be given greater weight than an informant with a low competency score. The answer key is the most culturally agreed upon responses for the dataset.

Visualization

One common way of visually displaying cultural consensus is through plotting informants via their first factor (competency scores) and second factor (residual scores) loadings (see Figure 5.4). To accomplish this, simply plot each informant along the x-axis by their competency scores and along the y-axis via the values from the second factor loadings.

EXERCISE: CULTURAL MODEL OF A BRAZILIAN MAN

Gender identity is a, if not *the,* primary way by which individuals are enculturated into different ways of being and behaving across. While gender is correlated with biological sex, it is distinct, being shaped and defined by cultural norms and expectations. The ways by which people "do gender," are varied, but often a society has a clear model of how one is expected to behave or not behave. Ethnographically, the dominant male gender role in Brazil is defined by *machismo*—a complex male gender role that emphasizes providing and protection of the family, as well as intramale competition and female sexual conquests. In a recent study, Dengah (2018) wanted to test this assumption, so he and his Brazilian colleague Ana Falcão first conducted interviews in order

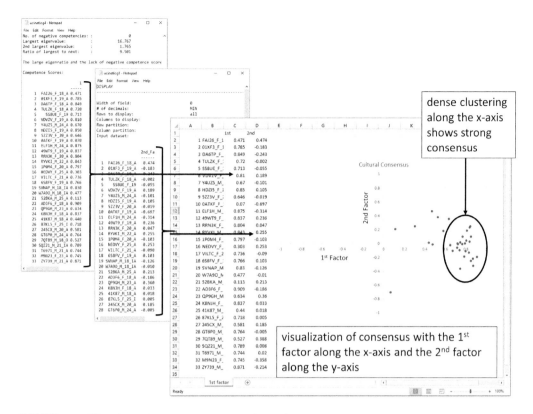

FIGURE 5.4 Visualizing Cultural Consensus Using *UCINET.*

to ascertain how Brazilians thought of widely endorsed gender roles. These interviews included free lists (as described in Chapter 3) and longer semi-structured interviews and schema analysis (as will be described in Chapter 7). Based off these interviews, 30 items were determined to be salient items of the cultural model the Brazilian man. A true/false cultural consensus question-naire was then created and administered, to verify the structure of the model and determine its cultural distribution. Please locate the supplementary dataset for this chapter (titled "Ch5_Brazilian_Male_Consensus_Data.xlxs") and open *UCINET.*

(1) First, let's get this data into *UCINET.* Take the *Excel* file that we've provided and con-vert/save it into your *UCINET* folder using that software's formatting (i.e., saving it as a *UCINET* four to six or seven format, which will create a file with a suffix like .##d, .##h, or .uci). Please be careful and thoughtful of where you save these files, for when you perform subsequent analyses on these data, you will be generating various output files as well. Good research means good bookkeeping!

(2) Once completed, take a quick look at the data. As with previous exercises, it can be good to take a sneak peek at the data, generate some initial observations, and then see how subsequent analyses reflect these observations (or not). Looking at this dataset in *UCINET,* (a) what do you see? (b) What kind of data are we working with here? (c) Do any potential kinds of respondents (and thus possible groupings) stand out?

(3) Now, we're ready to perform a consensus analysis. Find the Consensus Analysis opera-tion in the Tools window (click Tools/Consensus Analysis). Then, insert your data into the "Input dataset" selection (click on that small box to the right associated with "Input

dataset" and choose the *UCINET* data file you previously saved). Also, click on the other boxes associated with Output competencies, Output agreement matrix, and Output answer key, and direct them to where you want to save those files when they're produced (those files will appear after you click "OK"). Before selecting "OK," look at the "Analytic Model" pane in the bottom right (remember, you may have to expand this command window in order to see all this panel's information and choices): (a) What model should we be using for this dataset? (b) And what would you want to use if using other forms of data? (c) What would you choose for "Type of Data"?

(4) We're now clear for performing a consensus analysis: hit "OK" and you'll receive some data in the form of a text document. Assuming everything worked okay: (a) What should you do first with this document? (Hint: Remember the comment about book-keeping.) Then, start at the top of this output document and look over the "Respondent-by-respondent agreement matrix": (b) What do you see in that matrix? Next, move downward in this output document towards the table displaying "Negative competencies," "Eigenvalues," and the "Ratio of the first and second eigenvalues": (c) What's the largest eigenvalue, and what does this mean in plain terms? (d) What is the ratio of the largest to next largest eigenvalue, and what does this say about the possibility of shared culture? Then, continue down the output document and review the "Competence Scores": (e) What do those scores mean? Finally, review the "Answer Key": (f) What does this tell us about this sample's understanding of what it means to be a "man" in Brazil?

(5) Let's now look at this data in another way, this time utilizing both our competence scores (respondents' loadings on the first factor) alongside some the data we have on those same individuals' second factor loadings. First, locate your "2nd Factor" file in your *UCINET* folder (after pressing "OK" in the consensus analysis, this file will appear in whatever you defined as *UCINET's* default folder; it will show up labeled as something like, "loadings_on_2nd_factor.##d"). Once found, you can open this using *UCINET's* "Matrix Editor" in order to then copy and paste this data into a separate *Excel* sheet, alongside each respondent's corresponding competence score. If you like, we've presented a template to help you in this in the *Excel* sheet that you've been using for this chapter's exercises (in that *Excel* file's second sheet, labeled "1st and 2nd Factor Data"). Using the first and second factor data, create a scatterplot in *Excel*, mirroring the example data that we showed earlier in Figure 5.4 (with the 1st factor on the x-axis and the 2nd factor on the y-axis). If you need assistance, we've created this scatterplot in the third sheet of the accompanying *Excel* file, entitled "Data and Visualization," where we've also pasted each respondent's first and second factor loadings. Now, look at the visualization that you've created: (a) What observations can you make from this? In addressing this question, you might think back to the previously discussed *UCINET* output (e.g., eigenvalue ratio, competence scores, etc.). Then, for comparison's sake, look at the example that we provided earlier in Figure 5.4 which also maps first versus second factor loadings in a scatterplot, in this case with a highly consensual cultural model: (b) What differences do you see between this practice data and that earlier chapter example?

CONCLUSION: CULTURE AS SHARED MEANING

Cultural consensus allows us to verify that the cultural knowledge we are collecting has a degree of emic or ethnographic validity. This measurement criterion (emic validity) was recently introduced by Dressler and Oths (2014), though it is based on the most basic of anthropological approaches (Goodenough, 1980). As a reminder, the emic approach is concerned with understanding a cultural practice from the point of view of the practitioners. When used to describe cultural practices or to create scales and measures, an emic approach stresses that the terms, phrases, and overall focus be situated in a way that are linguistically and culturally meaningful to the population in question. Emic validity, therefore, assesses the extent that the data collected by the researcher does in fact reflect some degree of cultural reality. And the cultural consensus techniques discussed in this chapter allow researchers to assess the extent that any ethnographically (or otherwise) derived measure is tied to the lived experiences of the people featuring in a given research study. As such, researchers move beyond postulating culture as an amorphous bundle of beliefs and practices, and instead ground the culture concept more closely in day-to-day realities. In the following chapter, we will learn how to use the cultural consensus model as a stepping-stone to assessing culture members' individual congruity with group belief and practice: what we'll call cultural consonance, which has been proved a fruitful predictor of a variety of behavioral and health outcomes.

6 Cultural consonance analysis

CULTURAL CONSONANCE ANALYSIS

The cognitive anthropological methods described thus far have been focused on understanding how individuals within communities commonly make sense of and think about the social and natural environment. Free listing, pile sorting, and cultural consensus analysis are methodologies for eliciting the shared knowledge individuals of a culture possess. Yet, as discussed in Chapter 2, cultural schemas and models are self-motivating; they are more than just ways of thinking about the world, they are ways of acting in the world and thus of trying to accomplish things (based on one's various motivations). This means we need to still account for a missing but crucial bit of information: *How does such shared knowledge, i.e. culture, manifest itself in behavior?*

In this chapter, we will discuss the theory and method of cultural consonance. In a cultural consensus analysis, the topic of the previous chapter, researchers account for how knowledge is shared among members of a group. By contrast, in a cultural consonance analysis, a researcher assesses the extent to which individuals approximate shared cultural models in their own individual beliefs and behaviors (Dressler, Balieiro, Ribeiro, & Santos, 2007). Simply put, the cultural consonance method allows researchers to assess individuals' adherence to group understandings or norms—that is, it provides a measure of cultural conformity, in a sense. It takes the shared model identified by cultural consensus analysis and asks individuals (through self-reports) if they enact this model in their own personal behaviors and experiences. Theoretically, cultural consonance is a framework that leads researchers to hypothesize that the better culture members approximate the ideals of their culture, the more integrated they are in society, and the better their health. Conversely, misfit or peripheral individuals, i.e., those who are personally dissonant in respect to societal norms, suffer from increased psychosocial stress and related illness.

While a more recent approach in anthropology, cultural consonance has its roots in the classic works of Durkheim (1897) and Bourdieu (1984) and has provided researchers with a paradigm shift within the field of what's called "biocultural medical anthropology" (e.g., see Wiley & Allen, 2009). In this chapter, we will discuss the theoretical background underpinning cultural consonance, in order to emphasize its importance to the field of anthropology, as well as to the social sciences more generally. In particular, we emphasize key studies of Dressler's research on cultural consonance. Following this, we will present some recent studies that have utilized this approach, particularly within the field of medical anthropology. And finally, we will conclude the chapter with detailed instructions for carrying out this approach for yourself, accompanied by practical exercises for you to try.

THEORETICAL BACKGROUND

To set the stage, cultural consonance, developed by Bill Dressler in the late 1990s, can be thought of as "the degree to which individuals approximate widely shared cultural models in their own beliefs and behaviors" (Dressler et al., 2007, p. 195). This definition puts forth two key components—first, the idea that consonance is dependent on the ability of an individual to understand, interpret, and approximate the contours of a cultural model; second, that these approximations can be seen in their beliefs and behaviors. Measures of cultural consonance locate individuals within sociocultural space—assessing how well they approximate widely shared norms (or rules) of the culture, and thus how well they conform to normative social expectations as compared to other members of the society. To put this another way, cultural consonance allows us to understand the role culture plays in shaping individual behavior, as well as its influence on individual social status, as that's defined from local points of view.

To this point, we have discussed how cognitive representations allow us to interpret the world around us, and that shared knowledge allows us to have a joint understanding of reality that allows for social living. We have also discussed how much of this knowledge is oftentimes unconscious and automatic and thus feels natural and intuitive (Sapir, 1949). So, when we speak of cultural consonance, we are asking how individuals act in relation to cultural knowledge. That is, we are fundamentally asking about behavior, and how it is patterned by cultural norms. Indeed, much of our behavior is dictated by the unseen forces of culture. Nearly a century ago, anthropologist and linguist Edward Sapir wrote:

> Even comparatively simple forms of behavior are far less directly functional than they seem to be, but include in their motivation unconscious and even unacknowledged impulses, for which the behavior must be looked upon as a symbol.

> *(In Harris, 1951, p. 298)*

Take for instance, the relatively simple act of knocking on a door (which is an example Sapir himself used in an earlier 1929 publication). Functionally, the knock does not open the door. Rather, it symbolically communicates to someone else, on the other side of the door, to open it. The knock is only successful if other people understand and acknowledge the symbolic information contained in the action. The point here is, first, for our understanding of cultural consonance theory, (nearly) all behaviors are shaped by culture, and therefore have symbolic meaning (see also Bourdieu, 1984). Second, an individual's participation and adherence to these cultural behaviors is unconscious and automatic (i.e., characteristic of Bourdieu's *habitus*). We act and react to the world as if it were "natural," "intuitive," or "common sense," rarely reflecting consciously on the meanings culture members assign a behavior. Rather, our continued participation in these patterns reproduces and perpetuates them. It would be remiss not to emphasize that not all people conform to these patterns in equal measure. Instead, it should be thought that the social environment creates challenges, which require certain culturally agreed upon solutions. Some individuals may be more adept at utilizing these solutions, whereas others, by choice (i.e., according to their unique individual biographies), by force (e.g., lacking the resources for enacting certain individually preferred behaviors), or by enculturation (e.g., having internalized a different set of values) enact alternative behaviors (see Harris, 1951).

The ability of an individual to live up to the dominant patterns—or cultural models—of their culture is not without consequences. In fact, the degree of congruence of an individual with their (social) environment can result in substantial and significant health outcomes. This is the basic premise of Person-Environment Fit Theory (P-E Theory) (Caplan, 1983; French & Kahn, 1962)—psychological and physiological stress arises when there is an incongruence between an individual and their environment. The various versions and interpretations of P-E Theory need not concern us here (e.g., objective versus subjective fit). Suffice it to say that research in this vein has shown that misfit individuals demonstrate higher levels of psychological, physiological, and behavioral stress (Caplan, Cobb, French, Harrison, & Pinneau, 1980; Harrison, 1978). By contrast, individuals who maintain a good fit with their environment show more positive health outcomes (Edwards & Cooper, 1988). As you can see, just as other organisms thrive when they are a fit and adapted for their natural environmental niche, so are humans in their culturally created environment.

Obviously, humans' cultural environments can be extremely varied. Yet, social status hierarchies serve as a good example of an important dimension of the cultural environment, which seem to have particularly strong impacts on health. In fact, social hierarchies are rather intuitive to us as a species (and as primates), as they are omnipresent, manifesting in everything from families, to book clubs, to workplaces. If one views a social hierarchy as an "environment," we find that non-human primates, such as chimpanzees and baboons, who excel at fitting their environment (i.e., having high status), exhibit less stress and greater reproductive success than more misfit or low status individuals (Sapolsky, 2004).

We find similar patterns among us human primates as well. Socioeconomic status (SES) is a measure of how well an individual or a household is positioned to succeed in our modern cultural environment. Based off a composite score of income, education, and occupation, SES is one of the strongest predictors of health outcomes (Adler & Ostrove, 1999). The wealthier and more educated one is, the healthier they are and the longer their life expectancy is. It was widely assumed that the mechanism for this correlation was not wealth per se, but what one was able to do with this wealth (e.g., access more medical care, improve diet, etc.). However, studies that have looked at the correlation between wealth and health have found that material and monetary resources do not fully explain this association.

The Whitehall study (Marmot et al. 1991) on British Civil Servants is widely considered the preeminent analysis that demonstrates how SES influences levels of mortality and morbidity, as well as showing that there is something symbolic (i.e., cultural rather than only material) at play as well. In a longitudinal study of British Civil Servants, Marmot found reduced mortality and morbidity rates for each increase of pay grade. So, this seemingly supports the SES-health correlation, and it indeed does. But what researchers found was that the improvements in health could not be attributed to better medical care—because the UK has socialized medicine, to which everyone has access. Similarly, the SES-health correlation was not entirely due to diet or other behaviors (e.g., smoking or drinking), which the researchers were able to control for via partial regression analysis (a statistical approach that allows the variance explained by "control" variables to be accounted for). Known influences on health, including age, sex, body composition, health-related behaviors, access to resources, and medical access, only explained one-third of the SES-health gradient, leaving much of the correlation unexplained (Pincus & Callahan, 1995; Wilkinson, 2000).

This unexplained variance led researchers to consider that the influence of social hierarchies on health may be less about absolute status and abundance of material resources than it is about the experiences and meanings (i.e., the cultural models) ascribed to one's perceived status. Singh-Manoux, Adler, and Marmot (2003) investigated the role of subjective socioeconomic status as a correlate of well-being. In an extension of the original Whitehall study, the researchers surveyed London-based civil service employees and asked, *"What is your status compared to others in your community?"* Singh-Manoux, Marmot, and Adler (2005) found that the subjective social status (SSS) was as good or in some cases a better predictor of health outcomes than traditional, objective measures of SES. In what the authors would call "Status Syndrome," the subjective appraisal of relative abundance or deprivation of status can shape the ability to live a lifestyle that is endorsed by society. You can think about this via the phrase, "Keeping up with the Joneses," which exemplifies the pressure to have the same benchmarks of status/class as your neighbors. The thing is, "keeping up with the Joneses" results in measurable and meaningful health consequences (Adjaye-Gbewonyo & Kawachi, 2012; Wilkinson & Pickett, 2007). The discovery that SSS is a more accurate predictor of health outcomes has enormous implications, and begs a couple key questions: *What are meaningful measures of status within a particular cultural environment? And, what are individuals basing the appraisal of their social ranking on?* (Hint: cultural domain analysis can provide us the tools of identifying shared cultural models of "status" for any community.)

To summarize this theoretical background for cultural consonance theory, keep these points in mind:

- Cultural models provide the unconscious motivations for our behaviors. As such, these behaviors have cultural meaning, beyond their "functional" purpose.
- These patterned cultural behaviors allow us to function as a social species. The power of these cultural behaviors is a product of shared understanding and compliance.
- Not all individuals, by choice or by force, can live up to these culturally patterned expectations. Individuals who conform to these expectations can be viewed as "fitting" their sociocultural environment.
- The better one fits their cultural environment, the better health outcomes they have. Conversely, individuals who approximate less the ideals of their culture have higher stress and negative health outcomes. Status hierarchies are a type of cultural environment that demonstrate large health impacts.

DRESSLER'S THEORY OF CULTURAL CONSONANCE

In his Brazilian research, Dressler questioned the application of foreign measures of "status" in a highly economically stratified and developing nation. *Are the items and behaviors that are indicative of middle-class lifestyle in the United States similarly held by members of another population? Are they equally salient across different social-economic spectrums?* To address these issues, Dressler found guidance within cognitive anthropology, specifically in the theory and method of cultural consensus developed by Romney, Weller, and Batchelder (1986). To elicit an emic understanding of social status, Dressler and his Brazilian colleagues (1996) asked members of four differently economically stratified Brazilian communities what consumer items and behaviors were indicative of a successful lifestyle. After performing cultural consensus analysis (the topic of Chapter 5), they verified the existence of shared knowledge around a dominant cultural model that was informing individuals' opinions and behaviors (and thus possessing what they referred to as, again, emic validity). They found that regardless of economic status, the ideal Brazilian lifestyle was framed as a modest but comfortable life shaped by basic consumer items such as a television, sofa, kitchen table, refrigerator, etc., rather than conspicuous consumption (Dressler & Dos Santos, 2000). Individuals were then asked how well their own lives approximated those characteristics the community identified as necessary for achieving this ideal lifestyle—a measure of cultural congruity that the researchers labeled "cultural consonance" (Dressler & Bindon, 2000; Dressler & Dos Santos, 2000; Dressler et al., 1997, 1998). When measures of cultural consonance of the middle-class lifestyle were combined with psychological and physiological measures, the research team saw that higher levels of cultural consonance were correlated with increased psychological health (decreased stress and depression) and also with improved physiological well-being (lower blood pressure), *even after controlling for SES*. To put it another way, they found that failure to meet the cultural norms indicative of a middle-class lifestyle resulted in greater levels of psychosocial stress and blood pressure, regardless of their actual means (Dressler et al., 1996).

Since the formation of cultural consonance method and theory in the late 1990s and early 2000s, Dressler and his collaborators have been developing and expanding this approach. A complete recapitulation of these studies is beyond the scope of this chapter, and the interested reader should refer to Dressler's (2017) recent book on the subject. But a few findings are worth pointing out. First, his research has shown that consonance shapes multiple health outcomes. For example, Dressler, Oths, Balieiro, Ribeiro, and Santos (2012) found that consonance with the aforementioned "ideal lifestyle" domain predicted informants' body mass. Unlike in the United States, where body mass is inversely correlated with social status (overweight and obese individuals tend to be poorer Americans), Brazil exhibited a different pattern that diverged by gender.

Men's BMI increased with greater consonance with the ideal lifestyle model. Women on the other hand, exhibited an n-shaped curve, with those with the lowest and highest lifestyle consonance exhibiting the lowest BMI scores, with moderately consonance women having the highest BMI. Ethnography helps explain these results: traditionally, Brazilian men showed their status through their waist line, as emblematic in the phrase: "the size of a man's stomach is a measure of the size of his bank account" (Dressler, 2017, p. 151). Women, on the other hand, were expected to live up to the body image epitomized by samba queens and immortalized in songs such as "The Girl from Ipanema." Thus, consonance with the ideal lifestyle predicted BMI (a health measure), but also tapped into other cultural models of ideal body type.

Second, Dressler identified convergence of consonance across multiple cultural domains as another important outcome of his consonance research. In a 2007 paper, Dressler et al. analyzed cultural consonance across the five different domains, including lifestyle, social supports, family life, national identity, and food. As in the previous studies, consensus for these various cultural models was found across SES-ranked neighborhoods. Interestingly, regardless of economic status (again showing that objective wealth only matters so much), consonance in one domain was correlated with consonance in other cultural domains. This correlation between models, according to Dressler et al. (2007, p. 213), shows a "tendency toward consistency in beliefs and behaviors across cultural domains." And just as in the previous studies, consonance across cultural domains (while controlling for age, sex, and SES) was associated with reduced psychological distress and greater well-being. Importantly, this convergence suggested a hierarchy of cultural domains— with these separate cultural domains of lifestyle, social support, family life, etc.—as contained under a superordinate cultural domain of what one informant labeled as *realizações na vida* or "life goals" (Dressler, Balieiro, & Dos Santos, 2017). This notion of a system of multiple (congruent, overlapping, competing) cultural models is something we take up below in our notion of cultural dissonance (Snodgrass, Dengah, & Lacy, 2014, which we describe in more detail below).

Finally, and third, many other researchers have utilized the theory and method of cultural consonance to help explain health patterns in many different populations. This approach has been profitably applied to research involving Brazilian Pentecostals (Dengah, 2014), online computer gamers (Snodgrass, Dengah et al., 2011), Tsimane horticulturalists (Reyes-García et al., 2010; Schultz, 2014), HIV+ women in Kenya (Copeland, 2011), Andean highlanders (Brooks, 2016), Hispanic migrants in Mississippi (Read-Wahidi, 2014), Chinese and Taiwanese populations (Chick, Dong, & Iarmolenko, 2014), and many others (e.g., Andrews, 2018; Chick, 2002; Dengah et al., 2019a; Fanany, Fanany, & Tasady, 2014; Garcia de Alba & Salcedo, 2002; Maltseva, 2015; Sweet, 2010).

SOME SUMMARY REFLECTIONS ON CULTURAL CONSONANCE THEORY

A quick trip down memory-lane can elucidate the phenomena of cultural consonance in more personal terms. Think back to high school (for some of us, this was quite some time ago). *What did it mean to be "popular" in your high school?* Undoubtedly there were different definitions, depending on what "clique" you were part of (e.g., band, soccer team, journalism club, etc.). But there was also a shared understanding among most of the students that some people were more "popular" than others. *But how did you know these kids were popular? And how did you know that everyone else knew that these kids were popular?* First, you would need consensus around a shared cultural model of what constitutes popularity. Second, and the focus of this chapter, you would need to know that some students live up to the popularity model better than others. (In my (Dengah's) high school, it was a complex combination of having the right friends, wearing certain clothing brands, good looks, and having the right combination of academic and athletic skills, with a dash of rebelliousness.) Now think about what happens when you failed to live up to this model—*was it distressing? How did it feel to wear off-brand clothing?* (Dengah's mother would never concede to buy him a $200 pair of JNCO jeans, which nearly ruined his life, or so he thought at the time.)

Or, how about when you got a zit on the tip of your nose? Many teenage existential crises arise out of a perceived lack of consonance with socially valued behavioral and physical ideals.

It is important to note that these relationships are not clear-cut, as the amorphous and ever-changing nature of what constitutes the boundaries of these cultural models can be difficult to ascertain. As Maltseva notes, determining the degree "the link between the individual capacity for internalization, cultural competence, and emotional health...is a complex one" (Maltseva, 2018, p. 1315). For instance, some students, due to their own individual personalities, are less affected by the *Lord of the Flies* atmosphere of high school. In other cases, some students may eschew widespread popularity by thriving in a counterculture. (Though it should be noted that even high school cliques such as goths, skaters, etc. still have their own subcultural models of "popularity.") Yet others may find themselves torn between several incompatible cliques due to their contrary social norms. (In the classic 1980s film *Revenge of the Nerds*, having an interest in computers was shown to be incompatible with being athletic, good-looking, or having social skills.)

A recent study on female Utah college students shows the influence of incompatible cultural models on psychological health. Dengah and colleagues (2019) found that being consonant in either a secular model of womanhood *or* a Mormon (i.e., conservative Christian) model of womanhood yielded positive mental health. However, those who attempt to be consonant in both have higher levels of stress, as the models are incompatible with one another. Basically, one model (the secular one) encourages the young women to get a degree and have a career, while the Mormon model emphasizes marriage and motherhood above all else. The women in the study found that it was stressful to live up to these incompatible social expectations simultaneously. (See the text box below for another similar example of cultural model conflict.) While cultural consonance as a theory and method bring more evidence to the table, there are still questions to be answered about the exact degree to which someone internalizes, understands, and acts on a given cultural model.

OUR LAB: DISSONANCE IN ONLINE GAMING

Working within the cultural consonance paradigm, and building off previous research of our own, we wanted to know the effects of not just matching shared cultural models, but what happens when someone is stuck between two competing worldviews. In our ethnographic experiences in virtual worlds, we have found that highly involved, passionate gamers are often stuck between the rules, responsibilities, and social expectations of their "normal" everyday lives and their virtual play lives and fantasy identities (Snodgrass, Dengah, & Lacy, 2014). In looking into these issues more concretely, we developed a research agenda to examine how not just cultural consonance, but also what we called *cultural cognitive dissonance* (to reference sometimes incompatibilities and felt conflicts between competing mainstream cultural and subcultural norms) are important factors that could impact mental well-being among highly involved gamers. Using free listing, small-sample surveys, and participant-observation, we first developed cultural models describing real- and virtual-world success from the point of view of our gamer respondents. Then, we distributed a larger survey to our gaming networks, in order to examine relationships between gamers' ability to reach and approximate these models (that is, to be consonant with them) and their mental health. We proposed two hypotheses. First, we anticipated that dissonance between a mainstream model of success and a gaming-centric model of success would result in highly involved gamers deferring to their gaming model to compensate for not approximating the beliefs and behaviors associated with success elsewhere. Second, and relatedly, we believed that gamers with higher levels of dissonance (that is, incongruity between a real-life model and a gaming model of success) would place higher value on a gaming-model and would show various psychological features due to this dissonance. We found evidence supporting both of these hypotheses.

CULTURAL CONSONANCE GUIDE

The cultural consonance method is less computer software driven (though a statistical program such as *SPSS* or even *Excel* is useful), with the largest challenges related not to software but to how to meaningfully contextualize one's interview questions and measures so that they match local cultural expectations. As such, we forgo the strict numbering and bullet-points of our previous software guides, instead relying on a more narrative exposition.

HOW TO WRITE AN INTERVIEW PROTOCOL

The trickiest thing about this method is to convert the cultural model answer key, derived from cultural consensus analysis, into a series of statements that will appear meaningful to respondents (for this discussion, see Figure 6.1). The goal is to assess respondents' degree of adherence (via beliefs and behaviors) to a shared cultural model (previously established via cultural consensus analysis). In Dressler's model of the ideal material lifestyle in Brazil, he simply asked if individuals owned certain household items (*Do you own a couch? Do you own a car?*). This resulted in a yes/no dichotomous answer scheme. In Dengah's study of Brazilian Pentecostals, beliefs were very important to the model of the ideal Christian. In his consonance questionnaire, he utilized Likert responses, and had informants agree or disagree with several statements: *I always pay my tithing in full; I am a god-fearing Christian.* In general, you would like a mix of positive and negatively worded statements (assuming that rating the importance of negative terms would make logical sense).

Data collection

The answer key(s) derived from consensus analysis become the basis for cultural consonance analysis. Often written as true/false or Likert responses, informants are asked how well they meet, enact, believe, or live up to each item deemed important to the model. This is the consonance scale. Note, as a general rule, items that were not found to be important to the model are not included in the consonance analysis, as their meaning is ambiguous: *Is the item not important, or*

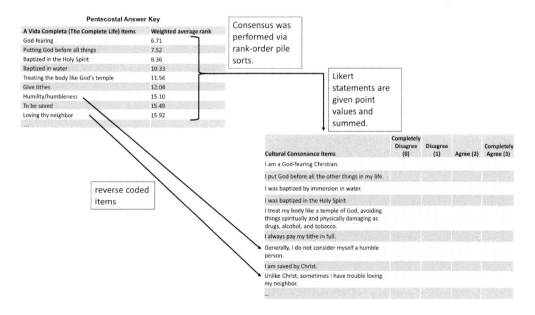

FIGURE 6.1 Creating Cultural Consonance Questions.

is the item the antithesis of the model? Prior ethnographic knowledge should help shape phrasing in the consensus phase to avoid such ambiguity.

Data analysis, part 1

Analysis for this method involves using a standard statistical program such as *SPSS*, *R*, *Stata*, etc. There are several ways to measure consonance to a model. The most straightforward way is to sum all of the items deemed important to the model: *more adherence equals greater consonance*. Most cultural consonance studies utilize this approach. A secondary way of calculating consonance is to weight each item by the consensus answer key (applicable for ordinal and interval data). Items deemed "very important" by the model receive greater weight than those only deemed "important." This is less used, as for many domains, the difference between "important" and "very important" is unclear or unimportant. Finally, most uses of consonance do not include items deemed unimportant to the model. Often, it is unclear if these items are the antithesis of the model or simply unimportant. If these negative items are wanted, consider using reverse coded questions during the interview.

Data analysis, part 2

With the consonance scale complete, correlations and other statistical analyses can be performed (see Figure 6.2). Generally, consonance is treated as a predictor variable, associated with various health outcomes. However, consonance can also be an outcome variable, shaped by other factors such as education, and personality traits (e.g., respondents' reported locus of control).

EXERCISE: GAMING INVOLVEMENT AND DEPRESSION

Cultural consonance analysis can be done with range of statistical analysis tools—e.g., *SPSS*, *Stata*, or *R*, rather than *Anthropac* or *UCINET*. (As such, this exercise presupposes familiarity with performing and interpreting basic statistical regression (for an explanation of this technique, see Dressler, 2016).) In the previous chapter, we learned how to generate a cultural answer key

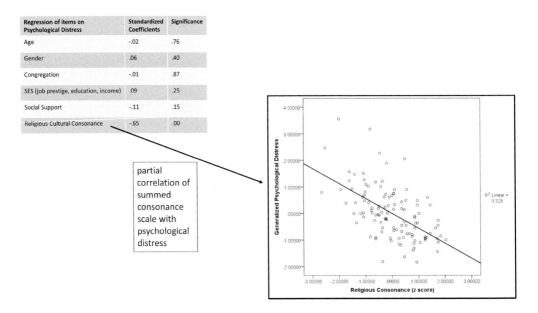

FIGURE 6.2   Analysis of Cultural Consonance (Using Standard Statistical Software).

from consensus analysis. In this chapter, we examined how closely an individual matches this answer key in their own belief and behavior results in a measure of consonance with the model. Further, we learned that consonance with a cultural model can impact an individual's well-being. Continuing along these lines, we are going to look at a dataset that uses this cultural model in order to draw conclusions about possible relationships between highly involved gaming and depression, an important topic in health psychology and other fields. First, find and open the accompanying supplementary *Excel* dataset entitled "Ch6_Gaming Consonance Dataset.xlsx."

(1) To begin, look over the dataset (as we always do both in these exercises and in our various research projects). (a) Based on what you see, how are these consonance data different than what we saw in the earlier consensus chapter and exercises? (b) What has changed about the way we elicited these survey responses?

(2) For this survey, we asked each respondent whether they felt each involved gaming item applied to them as a "yes" or "no." For the purposes of this demonstration exercise, we wanted to keep our examples simple. But, say, you wanted to recreate this survey but with greater detail and precision in the responses: (a) How else might you ask these questions? (b) And why might some research questions need more survey responses?

(3) Now that we've taken a few minutes to look at this data, and to think about how it was elicited, let's dig into it. As stated earlier, one quick method of viewing how consonant an individual is with a given cultural model is to simply tally how many model items respondents agree apply to themselves. For simplicity's sake, let's assume that an earlier cultural consensus analysis determined that the "correct" response to each item in this culture is "true." Thus, answering "yes" to these items (in the consonance phase of research) would mean that a respondent is more in line with the group's culturally shared consensual model of a highly involved gamer. (a) Tabulate the number of "yes" responses for each individual and thus their cultural consonance (either via a quick formula in *Excel*, through a statistical program like *SPSS* or *Stata*, or, the old-fashioned way, by hand! (ouch)).

(4) In this example, the culturally correct answer to each item was "yes," but they might just as easily have been a mixture of yes and no, as in a true/false exam in a class. (a) If that was true, how might this change the way you tabulate responses when calculating respondents' consonance scores? (b) Or, how might you initially frame survey questions differently if the "correct" cultural response is not an affirmative answer, and thus a more consonant individual reports that they do not personally embody the given item? Might it feel more "natural" in some instances to change the question format?

(5) Once you have summed the number of consonant responses from each survey respondent, take a minute to think about what these "consonance" scores mean. For comparison, look at Jeremy and Eliza. (a) What do Jeremy's responses indicate about him and his relationship to this cultural model, as compared to Eliza?

(6) Let's expand our scope to think about all of the respondents now: (a) Do you see any groups with differing patterns emerge? (b) What might be the reason for groupings to occur?

(7) The *Excel* spreadsheet also shows each respondent's depression score (in the column just next their consonance score). For the purposes of this exercise, assume that respondents answered 15 "yes/no" questions related to depression, with each affirmative answer reflecting that they experienced a depression symptom of some kind (with each item coded "1" for "yes" and "0" for "no"). The depression sum scores can thus range from 0 to 15, with a higher score indicating greater depression. (a) By simply looking at depression scores and at consonance scores, do you see any patterns? (b) How might you explain what you see?

(8) To formally examine patterns in the relationship of respondents' gaming involvement and depression scores, we're now going to do a regression analysis. Regression, briefly alluded to earlier in the chapter, is a statistical method for describing the relationship between an outcome of interest (say, depression) and one or more predictor variables (in this case, cultural consonance with this study's gaming involvement model, though we could add control variables like age, gender, ethnicity, hours gamed per week, type of game played, etc.). In the most common form of regression termed linear regression, which we'll employ here, researchers plot their pairs of values for their predictor and outcome variables, with the predictor on the x-axis and the outcome on the y-axis. Then, they use regression analysis to see how well a straight line describes this relationship. For example, as consonance gets larger, does depression tend to get smaller? Regression analysis does this in a detailed way, using a straight line to fit the plotted points. This makes it possible to take advantage of what is known about the equation of a straight line, as you would have studied in algebra course. Regression analysis enables us to use the slope of the line fitting our plot of points to summarize how one variable (on average) changes as the other changes. So, here, regression would let us be able to talk about how much of a change in a respondent's depression score is typically associated with (say) a one-point change in the consonance score (what's called the beta coefficient, though also referred to more simply as a regression coefficient or slope coefficient). Regression analysis is common to almost all data analysis packages, including *Excel* (though Dengah uses *SPSS* and Snodgrass *Stata*).

With this knowledge in hand, we will regress this study's depression measure (the outcome or Y-variable) on consonance with the involved gaming model (the predictor or X-variable). (If you're having difficulties performing a regression analysis, we've provided you with the statistical output (see the *Excel* file's second sheet).) (a) What is the beta coefficient, and what does that mean? (b) Is that result statistically significant, and what do you interpret that to mean? (c) How much variance in the outcome is explained by the model, and what new information does that provide? (d) More generally, does this analysis allow you to draw larger conclusions about the relationship between depression and cultural consonance? Explain.

(9) To aid in interpretation of a regression analysis like we've just walked through, researchers sometimes visualize in a scatterplot relationships between outcomes (here, depression, plotted on the y-axis) and predictors (such as cultural consonance with the involved gaming model, the x-axis). Again, common software such as *Excel*, *SPSS*, *Stata*, *R*, etc. can be used here. Go ahead and produce a scatterplot representing this study's key outcome and predictor in a scatterplot. (Or, look at how we've done that in this chapter's *Excel* dataset, sheet 3.) (a) What do you see? (b) Does this help you interpret the data and thus advance your understanding of the relationship between depression and cultural consonance?

CONCLUSION: THE CULTURE INSIDE US

Culture is self-motivating. Consider how omnipresent, and therefore oftentimes invisible, the hand of culture is in shaping, constricting, and channeling not only our thoughts, beliefs, and values, but also our motivations to act and thus our behaviors. Indeed, this is the *raison d'être* of culture. Social interactions of all types, from interpersonal communication to the functioning of entire societies, are predicated on the basis of culture members having shared understanding of the world, as well as individuals conforming to the standards and expectations of the group. Certainly, individual variation in thought and behavior occurs: individuals march in some ways to beat of their personal drummers, so to speak; but doing so is not without repercussions, say, in the form of social sanctions. Sometimes divergence with sociocultural norms can lead towards satisfying self-expression and innovative culture change. More than often, such divergences are met with social criticism (sometimes in the form of almost invisible "micro-aggressions") and even ostracization. Social psychology tells us that there is likely an evolutionary basis for such herd mentality—it is safer to be with the group than on the periphery; and organizations where everyone can predict each other's behaviors are more stable and healthier than unpredictable groups. Cultural consonance, as an emically valid measure of cultural conformity, provides a step toward understanding how adherence (or lack of adherence) to culturally sanctioned norms can help researchers better explain both human behavior and also mental and physical health outcomes.

7 Text analysis
Cultural models (and beyond)

Up until now, we have focused in this book on methods used to identify the content and structure of shared thinking within a group about a given topic (we have referred to those topics as "cultural domains"). The methods have related to eliciting interrelated words and phrases (free lists and pile sorts) and sometimes also propositional statements (cultural consensus and consonance analysis) related to a given facet of reality, which serve as useful proxies for the more complex understandings that individual group members have about the topic. But cognitive anthropologists have also developed tools for deriving underlying cultural understandings from qualitative texts such as interviews or stories (Bernard, Wutich, & Ryan, 2017), which are the focus of this chapter.

On the surface, what we described in earlier chapters and what follows in this chapter may seem quite different to readers. For example, in Chapter 5, we presented a formal method for determining whether or not there is consensual thinking within a group about a given topic. Here, we'll present a less systematic interpretive form of textual analysis aiming to illuminate how individuals differentially deploy cultural understandings, but with no simple algorithm or formal method for determining the degree to which discrete ideas are shared or not. Indeed, some researchers have explicitly stated that cultural consensus analysis (the focus of Chapter 5) and analysis of qualitative texts like narratives for their cultural models content (like we discuss here) are incompatible, given their different assumptions about how knowledge is stored in the mind/brain (e.g., as propositions, according to consensus analysis, or as schemas, in narrative approaches) (Garro, 2000).

However, we will demonstrate in this chapter how approaches like cultural consensus analysis are quite compatible with analytical strategies for eliciting cultural models content from qualitative texts like interviews. As in earlier chapters, we will again focus on eliciting shared cultural knowledge from language and speech, while also helping investigators appreciate the extent to which thinking within a group varies (to greater or lesser degrees) from individual to individual. Though the methods we describe here look different compared to earlier techniques we covered, we would encourage readers to be attentive to the distinction between cultural knowledge and the various techniques researchers use to elicit and assess that knowledge from respondents. Formal consensus analysis, for example, relies on assessing respondents' judgments (in "yes/no," etc. formats) about the "cultural correctness" of propositional statements about some domain of knowledge. Analysis of texts for cultural models, as readers will see, entails identifying in more complex qualitative texts (like interviews) respondents' shared thinking about a domain of understanding. But we shouldn't confuse the underlying cultural knowledge with the various analytical strategies researchers employ to measure and evaluate that knowledge—to do so would be to commit a fallacy associated with "operationalism" (where a concept is equated with its measurement).

To put a finer point on this, we do not conceptualize items on a cultural consensus questionnaire as exact equivalents of actual cognitive structures. Rather, such survey items, like the cultural consensus eigenvalue ratio, competence scores, and answer key used to summarize respondents' judgments about those items, are proxies and thus best estimates or schematic representations— that is, analytical models—of more complex underlying cognitive structures and neural processes. The same can be said of qualitative interviews, and our cognitive anthropological analysis of them, which also provide simpler cultural model summary proxies for knowledge that is more complexly arranged both in individual minds and at the group level. Based on the knowledge they possess, and the social settings they inhabit, individuals reason, make inferences, and even act in particular ways. As analysts, we attempt to better understand that thought and behavior based on how informants respond to survey items and/or report their knowledge and practice in a qualitative interview. Nevertheless, we remain keenly aware of the invariably more complex underlying cognitive and cultural organization of knowledge that remains beyond our ability to fully grasp and then represent to an audience. And we encourage readers of our book to remain analytically humble in this way as well. (For more on these points, see D'Andrade, 1995; Dressler, 2017.)

Overall, we focus once again in this chapter on socially transmitted and shared frames of meaning—what we've been calling throughout this book cultural models. Nevertheless, the foundation of the textual analysis approach we pursue in this chapter also rests on what has been called "theme analysis"—with *themes* roughly defined as discrete ideas or concepts expressed in speech, texts, films, paintings, and the like (Ryan & Bernard, 2003). In our cognitive anthropological parlance, we refer to those themes that can be held or "chunked together" in working memory as schemas (D'Andrade, 1995)—abstract mental representations of the world that interrelate a set of traits to form discrete cognitive objects that help us reason about a domain of understanding, as in the case of a bird schema tying together traits like *has a beak, wings, and feathers, flies, sings,* and so forth. However, we focus this chapter's analysis on cultural models, which, again following D'Andrade, are cognitive objects that are larger and more complex (D'Andrade, 1995; see also Dressler, 2017)—that is, cultural models, as we conceive them, are integrated sets of themes or schemas encoding a larger amount of shared knowledge, which again helps members of groups reason about particular things, persons, and processes in the world.

We believe that cultural models form a particularly sweet spot for the kind of textual analysis we describe in this chapter. Cultural models lend themselves to identification in speech events such as interviews, which, once transcribed into texts, are themselves complex and somewhat unruly. Despite this, cultural models can still be identified as discrete and manageable cognitive objects, which, when further related to antecedent causes and resulting effects, can form a firm foundation for even more complex analysis of cultural theories (D'Andrade, 1995), or even for "grounded theory" approach to textual data (Glaser & Strauss, 1967; see also Bernard, Wutich & Ryan, 2017). Though the latter textual analysis tradition is not the focus here, we show briefly in discussing our own research with gamers—focusing on their understandings of productive and detrimental responses to failure—how a cultural models approach is compatible with grounded theory.

In what follows, we first present classic work within the cultural models tradition of textual analysis, focusing most on Naomi Quinn's famous analysis of Americans' cultural model of marriage (Quinn, 1987, 2016; Strauss & Quinn, 1997). This is followed by a box insert of our own analysis of North American gamers' understandings—and cultural models—related to what they view as productive and detrimental responses to failure. We then present readers with a brief introduction to *MAXQDA* (https://www.*MAXQDA*.com) (Kuckartz, 2007), the main tool we use in our lab for managing and analyzing qualitative data such as interview transcripts, in the form of a guided tour of that software. This is followed by practice activities and exercises using that program. We conclude with some reflections on cognitive and cultural complexity, which sets up the final substantive chapter in our book, on personal network analysis and what we refer to as a "sociocognitive" approach to cultural analysis (de Munck & Bennardo, 2019).

Before proceeding further, readers should know that *MAXQDA* is not free of cost, but it can be downloaded for free during sample trial periods, the details of which are found on the software's website. Though we rely on *MAXQDA* in the current analyses, we would note that many of the lessons and techniques described for use in *MAXQDA* are translatable to other, similar qualitative data analysis tools, with which readers could also experiment.

AMERICAN MODELS OF MARRIAGE

In foundational cognitive anthropological work, Naomi Quinn conducted in-depth interviews—an average of 15–16 hours of taped conversation in each case—in the 1980s in North Carolina with husbands and wives in 11 marriages (Quinn, 1987, 2016; Strauss & Quinn, 1997; see also the discussions of this work in Bernard et al., 2017; D'Andrade, 1995). From her analysis of the transcribed interviews, she elicited what she called an American cultural model of marriage. The model consisted of eight major characteristics of marriage, as seen from the point of view of her respondents, which, Quinn argues, exhaustively accounted for all the hundreds of metaphors her respondents used when speaking about marriage. These eight characteristics were: 1. *Sharedness*; 2. *Lastingness*; 3. *Mutual benefit*; 4. *Compatibility*; 5. *Difficulty*; 6. *Effort*; 7. *Success or failure*; and 8. *Risk*.

Quinn's textual analytical technique consisted of identifying key words and phrases used by her respondents to talk about marriage, categorizing those key words and accompanying metaphors into (the above eight) overarching concepts, and generally paying attention to how such concepts shaped her interviewees' reasoning about marriage. In the terminology of this chapter, we would refer to each of Quinn's eight identified concepts as themes—discrete concepts expressed in speech (Bernard et al., 2017; Ryan & Bernard, 2003). But importantly, those concepts are grouped together to form a more complex yet unified schematic cognitive object—a cultural model—that shapes her respondents' thinking in regard to the cultural domain of marriage. As D'Andrade puts it,

> This model of marriage contains not only the standard American understanding of what marriage is—a love-based relationship in which people share their lives with the hope that the relationship will be a lasting one despite the difficulties of trying to maintain mutual benefit—but also a guide or map to what has happened, is happening, and may happen in the future to oneself and one's spouse.
>
> *(D'Andrade, 1995, p. 170)*

In related work, D'Andrade (2005) himself uses what he calls "gist propositions" to describe the content of cultural models. For example, in what he calls "The American Model of Society," the first four of his 16 such gist propositions in this domain, derived from extensive textual analysis of interview data with North Americans, are:

> 1. There are different levels of American society based on wealth and social status. 2. In America people move up (and down) these levels. 3. Success means either moving up (getting ahead) or staying at the top levels. 4. Money and social status motivate people to try to succeed.
>
> *(D'Andrade, 2005, p. 97)*

Quinn's and D'Andrade's approaches provide an instructive contrast about how to analyze text in order to illuminate underlying cultural models guiding thinking in a domain. Quinn's approach focuses on interrelated key words, phrases, and metaphors, which hearkens back to our Chapters 3 and 4 on free lists and pile sorts, where single words and phrases were typical of the examples we gave. By contrast, D'Andrade's analytical focus on full propositional statements about the world is closer to what we presented in Chapters 5 and 6 on cultural consensus and consonance analysis, where we more typically referenced examples employing statements about the domain in question. The point is that there is no single way to represent the underlying cultural model shaping thinking in a given domain of understanding. Analysts can use single words and phrases related to the cultural domain, full and grammatically correct propositional statements about the domain in question, or both. Yet, both are examples of *grounded theory*, inductive and ground-up explanations of cultural phenomena (Glaser & Strauss, 1967). Importantly, however, practitioners should always keep in mind, as alluded to earlier, that such representations are in the end simpler proxies for more complex underlying thought—a way to communicate the content and the structure of the cultural model to others—and thus not equivalent to the actual structure of knowledge in the human mind.

OUR LAB: VIDEOGAMES AND THE ART OF FAILURE

In a recent study (Snodgrass, Clements et al., 2020), we wanted to clarify causal pathways connecting individuals' cultural consonance with normative definitions of success and failure, on the one hand, and those respondents' mental wellness, on the other. We anticipated that positive and negative emotions such as pride, shame, and guilt might play critical roles in mediating between individuals' experiences of consonance with culturally defined success models and those individuals' experiences of mental wellness. For example, meeting important others' expectations might instill a feeling of pride, which could bolster positive wellness. By contrast, failing to meet others' expectations might produce shame or guilt, potentially contributing to depression or anxiety.

But as good cognitive anthropologists following the principles we describe in this book, we wanted to understand this phenomenon in local cultural terms. We developed an interview protocol, which allowed local gamers to speak about their experiences of success and failure, along with their accompanying emotions. Here are a couple of items from our interview protocol:

Think of an instance of when you failed at something: describe the situation.

How did you feel about this situation and your failure? Describe your emotional experiences in as much detail as you can.

Student research collaborators enrolled in Snodgrass's seminar at the time (spring 2019) coded their interviews for meaningful themes using the software *MAXQDA*. Initial analysis showed convergence in what our respondents considered productive as opposed to detrimental responses to failure—for example, in our respondents' parlance, learning and growing from failure, rather than dwelling on failure—with these two sets of themes becoming a focus of subsequent analysis. In addition to learning and growing from failure, which was the most salient positive theme from our interviewees' points of view, other common productive responses to failure included: taking responsibility for the failure, viewing the failure as an opportunity, practicing to get better, seeking support from others, asking for help, talking out the failure with others, and laughing off the failure. Along with dwelling on the failure, which was the most salient negative theme, other prominent detrimental responses included: stop trying, obsessively trying to fix the failure, blaming others, blaming oneself, keeping to oneself, using substances, self-medicating, and lowering expectations. Seeking distraction from the failure in other activities and avoiding thinking about the failure were viewed ambiguously, with some respondents thinking of them as a positive response to failure, others negative.

Each of these lists are cultural models of a kind: that is, socially learned frameworks of meaning that reflect (and potentially shape) gamers' thinking and experience related to how to productively as opposed to detrimentally handle failure. Further, each of the models joins numerous themes into relatively unified, if complex, cognitive objects. As Quinn and D'Andrade showed in their own analysis, a cultural model's individual items—its themes— often illuminate deeper underlying processes that join the various themes together. This analysis led us to the idea that our gamer respondents saw videogame play as potentially providing psychosocial resilience to failure and its negative emotional fallout (see Juul, 2013). That is, videogames, if played in the right "productive" way could provide gamers with a key source of resilience in the face of life failure and psychosocial stress.

We have described our lab's gaming research in order to detail the potential of a cultural models form of textual analysis. Also, we have aimed to show how such analysis can be integrated with the cognitive anthropological approaches described in earlier chapters (3–6), as well as with broader perspectives in the behavioral sciences, including what's been called theme analysis and grounded theory approaches to textual data. As we see it, a cultural models approach can usefully illuminate interconnections between disparate themes. For our lab's video game research, this included themes related to socially learned cultural models of productive and detrimental responses to failure. Further, in more complex grounded theory approaches (and also *content analysis*, as we argue in Snodgrass, Clements et al., 2020), cultural models can be shown to be cognitively and experientially related to antecedent causes (such as learning productive responses to failure through videogames) and succeeding consequences (becoming more emotionally resilient to failure by practicing more productive responses to failure). Overall, we hope the analysis presented here clarifies the potential of a cultural models form of textual analysis to address fundamental questions about human thought, experience, and behavior, in ways that segue neatly both with other cognitive anthropological analytical techniques, as well as with perspectives in the broader behavioral sciences.

SOFTWARE GUIDE: *MAXQDA*

INTRODUCTION

Qualitative texts can be derived from many sources: from interviews, of course, but also from phone call transcripts, internet forum posts, and the media (e.g., film scripts and other content, magazine and web articles, etc.). When it comes to analyzing qualitative data, there are tools available today that can assist researchers. A piece of software that we have used extensively and have taught our students to use is *MAXQDA*, a program with a range of features useful for managing and analyzing qualitative texts. Here, we will outline within *MAXQDA* basic steps, strategies, properties, and (what we might call) cognitive anthropological tricks, which we hope will help you advance in your understanding of the process of how to manage and analyze qualitative texts for cultural themes and even for full-fledge cultural models. Specifically, we'll run you through processes related to: (1) importing data into *MAXQDA*, (2) creating and coding segments of textual data, (3) retrieving and viewing specific coded segments, and (4) performing initial analyses and visualizations on texts. To ground our exposition, we rely on fieldnotes collected by Snodgrass's students in his methods seminars—these data come from actual field research, but names and likenesses have been changed.

While we focus only on the basics of analyzing qualitative data, you might find *MAXQDA* useful and want to learn more about its advanced features. For that, extensive guides and handbooks exist both online and in print (for many of these, consult *MAXQDA*'s own website, https://www.*MAXQDA*.com). Importantly, and as we said earlier, while we focus on *MAXQDA* in this handbook, the principles we describe are common analytical techniques, which can be employed in other qualitative data analysis software, such as *ATLAS.ti*, *Dedoose*, and *NVivo*. For example, the process of creating codes, retrieving coded segments, and performing analyses on coded segments are conceptually similar across these software platforms. If you do choose to utilize different software to perform your qualitative analyses, be sure to start by consulting the dedicated user guides, tutorials, and forums that cover many of the basics, as we do here for *MAXQDA*.

Also, readers will undoubtedly note that we organize this software walkthrough and exercises somewhat differently compared to similar sections in earlier chapters, in part due to the complexity of textual analysis, and the multi-functionality of *MAXQDA*. Specifically, we begin by describing *MAXQDA's* basic functionality, with those descriptions linked to software visualizations. There, we also encourage readers to open *MAXQDA* and run through some of the procedures we describe. This is followed by practical exercises, which we divide into two parts. In the first part, we describe again basic *MAXQDA* functionality, but this time in a way that is even more closely tied to practice activities for readers to do themselves. Readers will see some duplication there of material covered earlier, but we think this can be helpful, again, given the many things researchers need to think about when analyzing qualitative data, and the many analytical choices *MAXQDA* provides. In the second part of the exercises section, we walk readers through more focused practice exercises, related to two of *MAXQDA's* visual tools, the Code Relations Browser and the Code Matrix Browser, which we've found particularly useful. We accompany these exercises with an answer key (found, as in earlier chapters, in Appendix 1; if you a want a preview of these *MAXQDA* visualization tools, glance at Figures 7.8 and 7.9). Overall, compared to similar sections in earlier chapters, in both the software guide and exercises, we describe *MAXQDA* operations in a richer qualitative manner, which is perhaps appropriate given the nature of this chapter's material!

INITIAL *MAXQDA* STEPS: THE DOCUMENT SYSTEM AND DOCUMENT BROWSER WINDOWS

To begin, open *MAXQDA* and (in response to the prompts that appear) either create a new project or select the one we've provided for you in supplementary materials (after you've stored it on your computer), which features in our descriptions of how to use *MAXQDA* (it's titled, "Ch7_1–64ANON_DataSet.mex"; note that the "mex" suffix is a *MAXQDA* label referring to its general file type that works across the software's various versions). (Note: *MAXQDA* projects save automatically in a "Backup" folder created when you download the software, but you can "duplicate" a project file in an alternate location by clicking "Project/Duplicate Project" in the topmost *MAXQDA* command bar.)

On creating a new or entering an existing project, one of the first things you might remark on is *MAXQDA's* four main windows (whose arrangement can be adjusted by clicking on View/ Screen Layout Manager): the Document System, the Document Browser, the Code System, and Retrieved Segments. Let's first look at the Document System, where you store a project's qualitative texts (as text editor documents you import (using MS Word etc.), documents you create within *MAXQDA* itself, or other multimedia files you import). Located above the Document System window are a series of buttons that have corresponding hotkeys and shortcuts pre-programmed within *MAXQDA*, which enable you to manipulate and alter the Document System. There, you can choose, for example, to Import a document, Create a document, or Activate previously created documents (more on "activation" of documents later). If you are working with a larger dataset, it may be useful to create Document Groups (sets of related documents as defined by some criteria). This can be especially useful if you are planning on performing different analyses on different groups of documents (e.g., sorted by gender, age, location of the research, etc.). You can create a new group by selecting the "New document group" icon in the Document System panel. (Figure 7.1 shows how to import documents into *MAXQDA*.)

Once imported, you can view documents from within the Document Browser, whose window appears to the right of the Document System in *MAXQDA's* default setting (remember, you can adjust the layout of these windows). Within the Document Browser window, you can edit each text by turning Edit Mode on or off with Ctrl+E in *MS Windows* (Command+E if you're using *MacOS*) or by selecting the blue pen and paper icon in the top right. There, you can also highlight text, add memos, and much more.

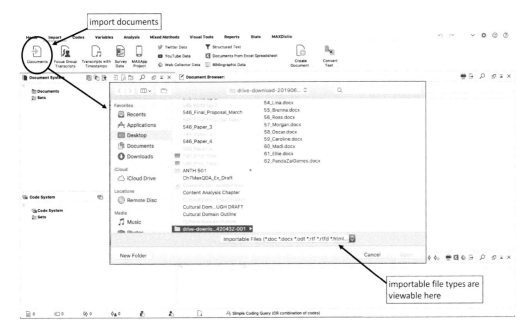

FIGURE 7.1   Importing Documents into *MAXQDA*.

When you've imported your documents and arranged them in a way that makes sense for you and your research project, or have decided to work with the dataset we've provided, it's time to learn about coding.

THE CODE SYSTEM WINDOW

Coding is perhaps the most important activity in qualitative data analysis. Codes enable researchers to assign meaning, value, and significance to text segments. Codes could relate to key themes you've identified, insights you think are important, features of speech that you detect in your data, and much more. The actual codes that you create will be influenced by how you want to approach the analysis and by your theoretical framework. For example, coding in inductive as compared to deductive analyses can look quite different, in terms of the unit of analysis, the number of codes created, and how you relate codes to each other. How to address these important issues will become clearer as we present specific research examples. For now, let's simply discuss how to create codes in *MAXQDA*.

First, find the Code System window, which is by default located below the Document System window. This is where you create all the codes you'll employ in your study. To create a new code, use the "New Code" icon (or Alt+N in *Windows*; from here on out, we'll reference *PC* keyboard commands, though know that *Macs* use different ones). In each instance, you need to assign a name (and ideally) a color to your codes. The name should be something memorable and specific enough to allow you (and your potential collaborators) to recall the code at a glance. You should apply the same or similar colors to related codes, which will eventually help you quickly perceive patterned relationships between codes in your texts. (See Figure 7.2.)

We'd recommend also creating a memo for each code. In *MAXQDA*, you'd type that memo in the box that appears whenever you create a new code (you can also right-click on a code to create or edit a code memo). In general, memos are notes you create for yourself (and again, also for your

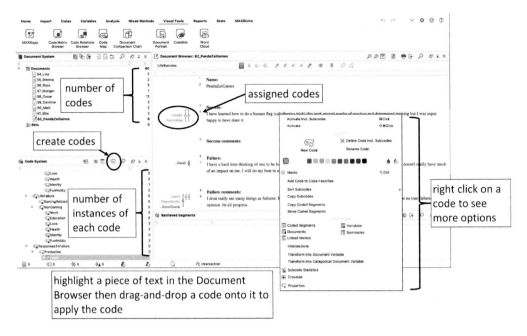

FIGURE 7.2   Creating and Applying Codes in *MAXQDA*.

collaborators). They take different forms, and we'll discuss others in due course. Code memos are helpful in that they force you to think more concretely about each code you create. A common code memoing practice is to define the code as clearly as you can, and to provide specific text examples that would be tagged with the given code (and perhaps also examples of closely related text excerpts that wouldn't be tagged). Once you've named, colored, and added a memo to your code, hit "OK," and you've created a code. As you create more codes, you can choose to link these codes together as parent and child codes: parent codes would represent larger, more encompassing analytical categories, while child codes could be used to specify themes etc. that are encompassed by the more general category. Considered all together, we'd call your system of codes, including each code's memo, your codebook, which are all located in *MAXQDA's* Code System window. (Figure 7.3 shows an alternate way to create a code memo.)

You are now ready to "code" text—that is, to apply a specific code to a specific text passage. To do this, first find a section of an individual (imported) text document (found in the Document Browser window) you think should be tagged with one of the project codes. There are several ways you can code sections of text: (1) highlight text and then click and hold the highlighted text and move this over to the code you wish to use, releasing when you are over the code, (2) click and hold the code that you wish to use and move this over to the previously highlighted text you wish to code, (3) click the "Code highlighted segment" icon in the top bar above the Document Browser, or (4) use the shortcut command Alt+C (the shorthand commands appear when you hover over an icon). If done correctly, the highlighted text will now display the name of the code and the color associated with the code in the left-hand column within the Document Browser. If you wish to delete the coded section, you can right-click on the code in that left-hand column and select "Delete" or use the "Undo code" icon in the top bar above the Document Browser (refer back to Figure 7.2).

Now that you have some coding basics, you might play around a bit, by creating new codes and tagging specific text passages with them. In later sections of this handbook, we'll discuss how codes can be usefully applied, and some things to avoid. But for the time being, go ahead and

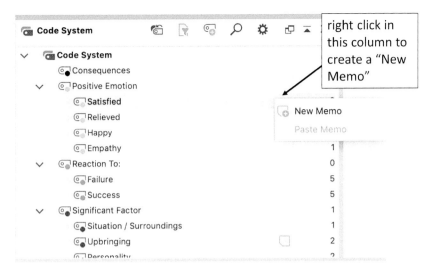

FIGURE 7.3 New Memo Creation in *MAXQDA*.

code passages from the *MAXQDA* project texts as you see fit, before moving onto the next section of this introduction—data retrieval, with results presented in *MAXQDA's* fourth and final main window, Retrieved Segments.

DATA RETRIEVAL; DOCUMENT AND CODE ACTIVATION AND THE *RETRIEVED SEGMENTS* WINDOW

As you develop your codebook and fill your project documents with colorful coded text segments, the next step is retrieving the coded text passages. Over time, you'll start to notice trends in your coding and analysis. For example, you may use one code more than others, perhaps eventually breaking it into numerous separate child codes. Or, you may notice that certain codes are often tagged to the same text passages. Whatever the case may be, retrieving coded text passages is essential for gaining a deeper understanding of the relationship between your codes and the text segments associated with them—a foundational piece of what we would call analysis of qualitative data.

In *MAXQDA*, the most immediate way of retrieving coded text segments is by double-clicking on a code in the Code System window. Doing so will open a new window that displays all instances of text passages you've tagged with that code. Examining what those passages have in common—and how they're different too—will help you clarify your current understanding of the data and perhaps give you insights into new analytical directions. For example, you might see the need for a separate code—or child code—based on what you see there. Note that clicking on any of the retrieved passages in that popup window will take you to the exact spot in the individual document (in the Document Browser window) where that passage appears. (Figure 7.4 shows retrieved coded text passages using this "double-click on the code" method.)

The second way of retrieving coded text segments requires using the Retrieved Segments window (see Figure 7.5 for what's described here). Here, we're going to do two things: first, we need to select (or "activate," in *MAXQDA's* language) the documents or document groups we want included in the retrieval process; second, we need to determine which codes within these document groups we want to retrieve. Notice how on the left of every document (in the Document System) and code (in the Code System), there's a small bubble. Clicking this bubble will "activate" the selected item for retrieval. Importantly, in this process, you must activate at least one document or nothing will be retrieved. Then, you can activate whatever codes you want to focus

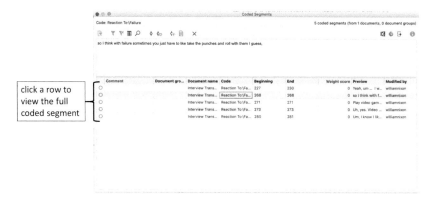

FIGURE 7.4   Retrieved Code Segments in *MAXQDA*.

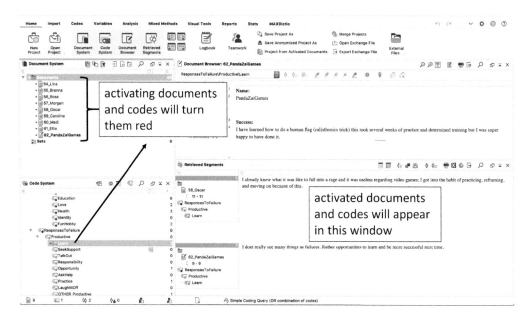

FIGURE 7.5   Code Activation and Coded Passage Retrieval in *MAXQDA*.

on within those documents. (As is probably obvious, you must also select at least one code (or child code), or no coded text passages will be retrieved.) The coded text passages associated with the activated document/code combination will appear in the Retrieved Segments window, where they can be examined in the same manner described above. Note here that clicking on any of the retrieved passages will again take you to the document where that coded passage occurs (in the Document Browser window). As a useful tip, you can choose to activate document groups individually in order to retrieve coded passages found only in those groups (as opposed to viewing all codes used throughout the entire Document System library).

Again, we would reiterate that the process of retrieving coded text passages, though simple to execute in *MAXQDA* (and other similar programs), is an important step in the *analysis* of qualitative texts. In retrieving coded text segments, you'll start to ask (and answer) important analytical questions: Are some codes only used only in certain circumstances? Are some document groups being coded more heavily with a specific code compared to others? How are codes associated with one document class being used somewhat differently in another? In the course of data retrieval, you'll start to answer these and many other questions, arriving at a deeper understanding of your qualitative data.

FURTHER *MAXQDA* DATA RETRIEVAL AND ANALYSIS TOOLS

As mentioned earlier, in the course of analysis, you'll start to notice that some codes co-occur with each other, being used to tag the same text segments. *MAXQDA's* "Complex Coding Query" provides a way to retrieve text passages that are tagged with multiple codes, in ways that you specify. Found within the Analysis tab at the top menu of *MAXQDA*, the Complex Coding Query tool first asks you to determine which kind of association you wish to utilize—e.g., in *MAXQDA's* language, "Intersection," "Overlapping," "If inside," "If outside," "Near," etc.—which you choose within the Complex Coding Query popup window, and which are visualized for you as well (see Figure 7.6). Before entering that window, you'll want to activate the documents and codes of interest for your query, which you can further manage (somewhat) within the popup window (e.g., choosing to work with all activated codes or just with certain ones). This form of analysis can be particularly interesting if you've developed a hypothesis about how or when certain codes would appear together. A complex coding query would pull up all the passages tagged with the codes you specify, in whatever documents (or document groups) you deem appropriate, and in the ways you specify (e.g., intersecting, etc.). Examining those text passages together might give you further insight into their relationships, which could also advance your analytical understandings of your data. We'd add that a query of this kind that yielded few results might force you to explain the absence of expected relationships, which could also advance your analysis. (Figure 7.7 shows a retrieved passage using the Complex Coding Query tool.)

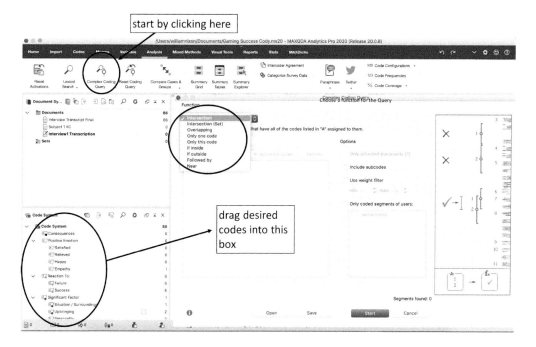

FIGURE 7.6 Performing a Complex Coding Query in *MAXQDA*.

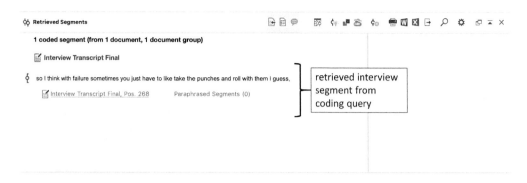

FIGURE 7.7   Complex Coding Query Output in *MAXQDA*.

A good way to get a bird's-eye of relationships between codes—and even between all the codes in your study—is the Code Relations Browser, found by clicking on "Visual Tools" in *MAXQDA's* top commands bar (see Figure 7.8). With this tool, you can see visually in a matrix how codes co-occur within a set distance from each other (e.g., for textual data, you can look for co-occurrences of codes falling within X paragraphs distance from each other), choosing to view these data numerically or graphically as icons (whose sizes depend on the number of co-occurrences). We think this tool can be useful in identifying links between themes, which you might conceptualize as schemas that in turn are linked together in a more complex cultural model. Using this command, you would expect to see such themes co-occurring with each other in the matrix, which

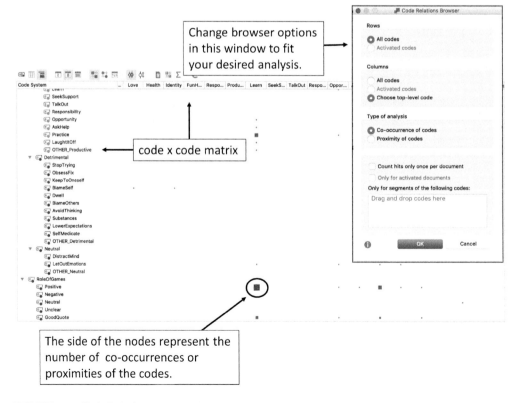

FIGURE 7.8   Code Relations Browser in *MAXQDA*.

would confirm that they were interlinked in some way in the form of a model. If you didn't, you would want to explain why, before proceeding further with that line of inquiry. (That's one of the cognitive anthropological tricks we mentioned earlier.)

Another way to get a good view of the co-occurrence of codes with each other is by using the *MAXQDA* Code Matrix Browser, again found in the Visual Tools tab (see Figure 7.9). Using this command, instead of viewing code-code co-occurrences directly, you see the number of times a code (or all your codes) appears in a given document (or document group). This can give you a sense of the themes—as tagged by specific codes—featuring, for example, in a given interview with a particular informant. But looking across informants, for example, you might notice that certain codes regularly co-occur with each other, thus giving you further insight into the relationships between codes. Again, this might be helpful in identifying how themes (as schemas) were interrelated—or not—in what you perceived to be a more complex cultural model. It might also point to the relative salience (or prominence) of certain schemas in the model. And if at least some of those themes didn't co-occur with each other in, say, a given respondent interview, or in multiple interviews, you might have to re-think your incipient cognitive anthropological analysis. Or, you might think more about why the model—or certain parts of the model—are more prominent in certain interviews compared to others. (More tricks?)

You'll want to keep cognitive anthropological questions like these in mind as you work through the *MAXQDA* activities presented in the next section.

EXERCISES: *MAXQDA*

PART 1—*MAXQDA* BASICS

As alluded to at various points earlier in the chapter, identifying underlying cultural models (and their schema components) within text is challenging, and we would add, even more so when done by hand. Before software like *MAXQDA*, some researchers printed out texts such as interview transcripts, cut them up into smaller labeled pieces, and then physically sorted those text fragments according to their themes (with the cutting and sorting process repeating itself as the

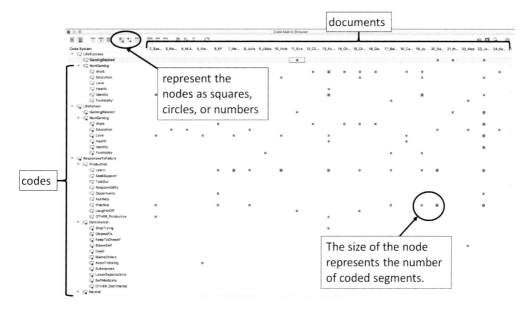

FIGURE 7.9 Code Matrix Browser in *MAXQDA*.

analysis progressed)—much like a pile-sort!, but without an *Anthropac* equivalent to help them. We hope that readers will appreciate the utility of *Anthropac* software in that earlier context. But we also hope that readers will similarly see how the software didn't do our analysis for us in the research examples discussed earlier. That required careful and informed thought, and ethnographic insight. For example, think back to the sound judgment and ethnographic knowledge required when making pile-sort decisions about how to combine (or not) similar terms into the same category in that chapter's involved gaming exercise. The same is true of *MAXQDA*. It's powerful, but it won't do your analysis for you.

That said, we have developed some practice activities and exercises to help you familiarize yourself further with *MAXQDA*. As alluded to earlier, in this first part, we walk you through some activities, but without formal exercises and answer key, which don't come until the second part. (In the first set of activities, we do italicize some sentences where we describe what you should see after performing the operations we describe, which is an answer key of a kind.) Again, you'll see some overlap between what we described earlier in our *MAXQDA* guide and what comes here, in large part out of respect for the complexity of qualitative texts analysis (and this software as well).

If you haven't already done so, download *MAXQDA*. (Remember, there are free trial versions of this software.) Then, find this chapter's supplementary dataset, which we referred to earlier in the software guide section ("Ch7_1–64 ANON_DataSet.mex"). This project consists of short text excerpts taken from open-ended questions in a recent online survey of ours, where we had videogame players discuss how they responded to life successes and failures (if you're interested, here's the survey: https://tinyurl.com/gamermodels. We coded these text excerpts according to the nature of the success and failure, and whether informants responded productively or detrimentally to them, with each of the latter parent codes containing numerous child codes, which were informed by earlier qualitative interviews. In our analysis, we sought to identify relationships between videogamers' responses to life success and failure and their game-play (for more detail, see Snodgrass, Clements et al., 2020).

MAXQDA INTERFACE

First, let's review *MAXQDA's* four main windows and their associated functions, which we discussed earlier:

- **Document System**—This is where a project's uploaded documents appear. As you'll see, we've already imported this project's texts—64 of them. But for practice, choose a file on your computer and upload it to this project. (Here, you might review Figure 7.1.) Uploading files into *MAXQDA* is straightforward. The software can import many different file types, but for our purposes we suggest you stick to text files in a *Microsoft Word* format (or in some other text editor format) rather than, say, an image or video file (which *MAXQDA* can also handle). Click on the "Import documents" icon on the Document System header bar and choose your file. Or, in *MAXQDA's* upmost command bar, click on "Documents" and choose "Import Document(s)," once again navigating to the file you want to upload to this project. (Remember, in *MAXQDA*, there are typically multiple ways—icons, menu commands, keyboard commands—to do things, though it takes time to learn the routines.) *You should see your new document appear at the top of the Document System panel.* Right-clicking on a document, like the one you just uploaded, will show a list of applicable commands for any of the project's documents. Practice by adding a memo to the new document you just uploaded by right-clicking and selecting "Memo." You might type in the text-box portion that appears in the memo popup window something like, "This isn't really part of this project!" *Close the memo window, and you* *should see a new memo icon just to the right of the document in the Document System.* (Note that you do not need to save this memo, as *MAXQDA* does that automatically. If you want to edit your new memo after you've closed its window, double-click on its icon.) Much like the earlier code memos we discussed, you can also add notes to documents to create document memos, in order to lend further context to that document. You will need to decide what would be helpful to have in such a document memo, though we've found it useful in projects using interviews to note things about the respondents (such as demographic factors or particular experiences that seemed to shape the interviewee's responses) or about the context and content of the interview itself (e.g., the setting of the interview, interviewer-interviewee rapport, etc.).

- **Document Browser**—Here's where the text for a selected document is displayed. Double-click on one of the documents in the Document System in order to bring it up in the Document Browser panel to the right. *You should see the Document Browser window populate with the document you've selected.* In the Document Browser window, you can highlight portions of text and assign them codes, which we'll walk you through again momentarily. For now, hover over the different icons at the top of the Document Browser window to see some of the different commands you can use. (Figure 7.2 shows all *MAXQDA's* four main windows, including the Document Browser pane, which appears top-right.)
- **Code System**—Codes that you create appear in this panel. As discussed earlier, we've created codes in this project associated with life success and failure, and productive and detrimental responses to such experiences. As also alluded to earlier, codes can be nested within broader parent codes that allow for more general or specific levels of coding. For example, our *ResponsesToFailure* parent code has *Productive* as a child code, which is itself a parent code to various forms of productive responses to failure, learned through our earlier ethnography and interviews, such as *Learn, SeekSupport, TalkOut,* etc. Hover the toolbar icons to view your different options in the Code System window. (See Figure 7.2, bottom-left, for this window.)
- **Retrieved Segments**—As discussed earlier, in *MAXQDA*, you "activate" codes and documents in order to make them the focus of certain kinds of data retrieval and analysis. Text passages associated with activated codes that are located within activated documents will appear in this window. Though we also talked about this earlier, we will again walk you through how to activate codes and documents later. (The Retrieved Segments panel features bottom-right in Figures 7.2 and 7.5.)

CODING

Start familiarizing yourself more with the project's individual codes and documents. Look through the already existing codes and read through a few project documents to get a sense of their content. This will give you a better idea of how you might yourself link a given code to a specific document's text passage. After reading through some documents, try to identify a new theme that stands out to you. If you're still having trouble conceptualizing what a theme is—and how to identify it—you might look back at this chapter's earlier "Videogames and the Art of Failure" text-box example, where we discuss the productive and detrimental responses to failure themes that feature in this dataset. Or, for a more in-depth treatment of the topic, consult Ryan and Bernard's (2003) guide.

Once you've conceptualized in your head a theme that you'd like to attach to a particular text passage, start by creating a code for that theme. As discussed earlier, there are multiple ways to do this in *MAXQDA*, but a fast and easy method is to click on the New Code button in the Code

System box (it looks like a price tag with a green plus symbol; you might refer again to Figure 7.2, where that icon is circled, for this and all subsequent discussions of coding). In the popup window that appears, you're able to give your code a name, assign a color to it, and write a code memo associated with it (for one instance of how to do create that memo, see again Figure 7.3). Go ahead and use this window to name and assign a color to your new code (you could also write a memo in that popup window's text-box, so that you remember what your new code means, or, so that a collaborator knows). The code you created should now appear in the Code System panel in the bottom left of your screen. Congratulations! You've created your first *MAXQDA* code (and first code memo). (Or, maybe not, if you created those during our earlier discussion.)

As we've discussed repeatedly, in programs like *MAXQDA*, you can nest more specific child codes within other broader parent codes in order to represent different aspects of that broader category. For example, in this project, you might want to create new child codes to represent additional processes that shape one's life success or failure, perhaps adding *Personality* to *Family* and *Upbringing*. Or you might want to create a new parent code, *FailureInfluences*, with its own corresponding child codes, *Personality*, *Family*, *Upbringing*, etc. Either using our suggestions or some other idea of yours, practice creating nested parent and child codes within the Code System window. *Those codes should also appear in the Code System panel.* Here, once you've created the parent code, you might right-click on it and select "New Code" from the popup menu. You will see the same window appear, but when the new code is created it will be nested under the original parent code. A quick and easy way to make child codes! Note also that you can move codes up and down in the system after clicking on them and dragging and dropping them onto the code under which they are to be nested. (A few more small tricks, though not narrowly cognitive anthropological ones.)

CODING TEXT SEGMENTS

Now, start assigning codes to text segments found in the project documents. To do this, first double-click on the document (in the Document System window) that you want to focus on, which will make it available in the Document Browser window. Then, in the Document Browser panel, highlight with your mouse the portion of the text in that document that you want to code. Then, drag and drop the applicable code onto the highlighted section of text. *You should see a color-coded bracket and the name of the code appear in the left-hand margin of the Document Browser window next to the new coded text.* If you haven't done so already, assign some of our codes and some of your own new ones to what you think are relevant passages in the project's various documents. (If you're having problems, you might refer once again to Figure 7.2.)

ACTIVATING CODES AND DOCUMENTS

As previously discussed, *MAXQDA* works well as a data retrieval tool once you have coded your documents. Practice retrieving text using the previously discussed code and document "activation" method. To practice doing this, first, right-click on the "Documents" icon (in the Document System window) and select "Activate All Documents" (see Figure 7.5). This command tells *MAXQDA* that you want to retrieve coded portions of texts from all the project's documents. (If you would like to activate just a single document, you can do so by right-clicking on it and choosing "Activate.") *All activated documents' icons should appear red.* The next step is to activate the code(s) that you are interested in finding within those documents. Similar to when working with the documents, you could right-click on the overarching "Code System" icon and select "Activate All Codes." Or, you could right-click on codes individually and select "Activate" in the popup menu. If a code has child codes, you'll need to decide if you want to activate those too by choosing "Activate incl. subcodes" (or not). *Activated codes also turn red. Also, once both documents and codes have been activated, all the corresponding text segments associated with that document-code combination will appear in the Retrieved Segments window in the bottom right of your screen.* Remember, if you click on any one of those retrieved segments, you'll be taken to its exact location in its corresponding document (in the Document Browser window).

PART 2—*MAXQDA* VISUAL TOOLS EXERCISES

As discussed earlier, *MAXQDA* provides researchers with multiple visual tools to help them better recognize patterns within their coded documents. Here, we'd like you to explore two of them, which we've found particularly useful: The Code Relations Browser and the Code Matrix Browser. For these exercises, you'll continue to rely on the same dataset used in the first set of activities ("Ch7_1–64ANON_DataSet.mex"). If you changed that project substantially in your earlier practice activities, you might download a fresh version of the project, to ensure that your analyses will correspond with our own.

CODE RELATIONS BROWSER EXERCISES

(1) As discussed earlier, *MAXQDA*'s Code Relations Browser allows analysts to visualize relations between individual codes in terms of the number of times they are used to code the same text segment (for this tool, see Figure 7.8). Navigate to *MAXQDA*'s top toolbar and click on "Visual Tools" and select "Code Relations Browser." This will bring up an options menu that allows you to tailor the analysis and output to your preferences. For this exercise, select "All codes" (both for Rows and Columns) and "Intersection (or Co-occurrence) of codes" for Type of Analysis. Leave the other options at the bottom unchecked. Click "OK," which will bring up the Code Relations Browser output screen. There, you will see a code-by-code matrix, with different sized nodular squares representing the number of co-occurrences of codes. Larger squares (or nodes, you can change them to appear as circles, numerical values, etc.) represent an increased number of times that any given code co-occurred in any coded text segments with any other code across all the documents in the project.

For this exercise, focus your attention on two of the rows (codes) near the bottom of the spreadsheet, *RoleOfGames/ Positive* (i.e., games are judged by survey respondents to play a positive role in their lives) and *RoleOfGames/ Negative* (by contrast, they are seen to play a negative role). (a) Which of these two codes was used more to tag text segments? (b) Which three cells in those two rows have the highest number? (c) How many times did codes in those three highest number cells co-occur with each other? (d) What do you interpret this all to mean? (You should be able to intuit the meaning of the shorthand code names, based on this chapter's descriptions of the research. The column variables are labeled in a particularly shorthand fashion, though you'll see there that a parent code column precedes (to the left) each set of its child code columns. Note too that the matrix duplicates itself above and below its diagonal. This means that you can look to the rows for each column's full parent/child code description. If the code meanings are still not clear to you, more detail is given in Snodgrass, Clements et al., 2020, and especially in that article's codebook appendix, which you could consult. Or, just do your best and then jump to the answer key, where we explain things.)

CODE MATRIX BROWSER EXERCISES

(2) Now, let's look at the Code Matrix Browser, which you can also find under the "Visual Tools" header in *MAXQDA*'s top toolbar (see Figure 7.9). For this part of the exercise,

make sure the Code Relations Browser is closed out in *MAXQDA* and then click on "Visual Tools" and select "Code Matrix Browser." This will again bring up an options window that allows you to specify what kind of output you would like to see. For the purposes of this exercise, select "Documents" (for Columns) and leave the other options unchecked. Hit "OK," which will bring up a matrix with different sized nodular squares, which looks similar to what we saw in the prior set of exercises. But this time, it's a code-by-document (rather than code-by-code) matrix, with each row representing a code and even column a document. The different sized squares show the number of times a code was used in a particular document, with larger nodes meaning more uses of the code in that document. Scroll through the matrix to get a sense of how frequently each code was used in the various documents. (a) What's the highest number of times a code was ever used in a single document? (b) In which two documents, were the most codes used? (c) What are the two most frequently used codes across all the documents? (d) More generally, what did you learn from this code-by-document matrix visualization exercise?

CONCLUSION: CULTURE FOUND BETWEEN THE LINES

In this chapter, we've sketched a cognitive anthropological cultural models approach to analyzing textual data such as interviews. This included reference to classic cultural models studies by Quinn and D'Andrade, as well as to our lab's own research on gamers' understandings of productive as opposed to detrimental responses to failure, and how such responses might shape emotions and even mental health. Finally, we presented a brief guide to *MAXQDA*, one of a family of qualitative data analysis and management programs, which we've found particularly useful for this kind of analysis.

On the surface, this chapter's content might seem to represent a break with earlier topics described in this book. As such, we've taken pains to demonstrate how the analytical aims in this chapter are continuous with earlier cognitive anthropological approaches (such as free lists, pile sorts, consensus and consonance analysis), and also with broader behavioral science textual analysis traditions (theme and content analysis, grounded theory). Similar to earlier chapters, the techniques described here can help researchers identify socially learned and shared cognitive patterns of thought—what we're calling schemas and models. Too, relating such patterns of thinking to ancillary causes and resulting effects can further clarify the role these cognitive objects play in regulating human thought, experience, and behavior, helping researchers build from the ground-up, and subsequently further confirming, social scientific theories.

The next chapter focuses on personal networks, seemingly another break in continuity with this book's focus. However, we'll illuminate how important it is to root patterns of thinking within social networks of interaction, building up what we refer to as a "sociocognitive" approach to human thought and behavior (de Munck and Bennardo, 2019), with further important implications for cognitive anthropological method and theory.

8 Personal network analysis

Humans are social and cultural animals, who function best when able to interact with others and learn from them. From the time that we're born, we're inundated with cultural knowledge. Through various forces of socialization and enculturation (e.g., family, schools, work, leisure groups, etc.), many of the models, schemas, prototypes, and frames that give meaning to the culture we inhabit take shape. Previous chapters of this handbook have shown how culture as knowledge can be identified through rigorous methodological techniques. It should be apparent, however, that this book's approach to culture as discrete (and multiple) knowledge structures is different from conceptualizing a monolithic Culture: each individual inhabits multiple social niches that require them to employ various forms of cultural knowledge. Even the most ardent and cloistered members of a cultural group today must navigate various norms, beliefs, and behaviors in order to give structure to their own life. This leads us to ask: *How might individuals negotiate competing cultural models? What impacts would the possible cognitive tension emerging from such negotiations have on them? And importantly for this chapter, where do these competing models originate?*

Social network analysis has emerged as a tool that allows researchers to learn more about the connections that we all create and navigate in our daily lives. Whom you rub shoulders with on the train, buy food from at the marketplace, and go to temple with imbues you with implicit and explicit cultural knowledge. As we begin to trace these connections, the patterns in which cultural knowledge is communicated comes into clearer focus. An individual's network could be dominated by one "majority" cultural clique (their family, for instance), but their secondary social groups (soccer teams or school friends) also contribute to their thinking and behavior. By delineating these cliques within a network, we can begin to make some claims about where cultural knowledge emerges from and how this impacts the individual's own conceptualization of culture.

In fact, what we discuss in this chapter relates quite centrally (and practically) to what came earlier in the book. For example, consider that in every cultural consensus analysis (Chapter 5), researchers are by default asking (either explicitly or implicitly) respondents to think about some domain of thought (e.g., forms snow can take, the meaning of addiction and life success, etc.) in reference to some particular social group: e.g., "How do members of your family/your close friends/people around here/mainstream society/etc. think about snow, addiction, life success, etc. ...?" We hope it's therefore clear that consensus analysis thus also implies thinking about the social network within which cultural knowledge is circulated.

This chapter, then, details how social network analysis can help us to more specifically locate culture in particular social relationships. It is not an entirely precise process to locate the social origins of certain cultural patterns of thought. That is, we cannot say definitively that a particular individual learned what it means to be a proper Buddhist from a particular individual or group. But network analysis does help us gain further clarity into how cultural knowledge is shaped and transmitted from individual to individual. The particular approach we describe here is called ego-centric network analysis, or personal network research. Here, we will be primarily concerned with how relationships and social cliques impact the individual: *how do these groups enact some cultural knowledge onto the person we're interested in?* This is in contrast to sociocentric or whole network analysis, where we'd instead be interested in knowing more about how an entire network is constituted, and how members within that network influence each other.

The following sections of this chapter will briefly outline basic theoretical assumptions that emerged to form the basis of social network analysis as a method. Case studies will then outline the ways in which egocentric network analysis can reveal how sociocultural information is shared and shaped by social connections. The chapter will then provide a guide for collecting and analyzing social networks, via the computer program, *EgoNet* (McCarty, 2003).

In going through this chapter's material, try to keep in mind how your own personal networks have shaped your understanding or knowledge of the world. *From where have you drawn most of your insight about the world? How have you been forced to think about the world differently when you've interacted with individuals holding different cultural models about how the world works? And what impacts might these interactions have had on your conceptualizations of the world you inhabit?* Also, as a researcher, start to think more about the implicit social network component of any cultural domain, consensus, or consonance analysis. *How might you best frame such studies' item elicitations? In relation to what personal network, e.g., family, friends, mainstream society, etc.? And why?* Try to keep questions like these in mind as you progress through this chapter covering egocentric (or personal) network analysis. Thinking through such questions will help you tie this chapter's content more closely to the book's earlier more exclusively cognitive anthropological approaches to culture.

THE TIES THAT BIND AND SHAPE US

The connections that individuals have in their networks can provide them with opportunities to achieve the goals embedded in cultural models. That is, social networks provide us with various forms of *capital* (i.e., resources, knowledge, and support) that allow us to behave in certain ways and enact particular lifestyles (Granovetter, 1973). By relying on and increasing the size or density of their networks, an individual may be better able to exchange, influence, understand, and realize the cultural knowledge found throughout this network. As a result, individuals who are embedded within large networks with strong bonds between individuals have better health outcomes. Purely in terms of social network size, research from Cohen and Wills points to the ability for individuals to potentially buffer stress by increasing their connections with others (Cohen and Wills, 1985). Similarly, Dressler and associates discuss "cultural consonance in social support" (CCSS) as being a vital aspect of connections to consider (Dressler et al., 2016). Utilizing this framework, Dressler was able to demonstrate how CCSS results in better psychological and physiological health outcomes (Dressler, Balieiro, Ribeiro, & Santos, 2007). Thus, both quantity and quality of social connections are likely to mediate an individual's ability to understand culture and embody it.

One interesting feature of social network analysis is the basic premise of *homophily*: the idea that "birds of a feather flock together," or that "like attracts like" (Aral, Muchnik, & Sundararajan, 2009; McPherson, Smith-Lovin, & Cook, 2001). People naturally tend to gravitate and become more similar as they exchange ideas, and enact cultural norms together, which is a phenomena that has received attention through various social conformity theories, such as contagion theory (see Christakis & Fowler, 2013; Sampson, 2012) and social comparison theory (Festinger, 1954). As such, the overall characteristics an individual's social network tend to reflect the characteristic of the individual, and vice versa—liberal people tend to have liberal social networks, gamblers will have more gamblers in their networks, educated people will have more educated friends. It should be little surprise that these networks can also imbue various health impacts on members within them, with evidence supporting the role of social network influence on addiction, obesity, and heart disease (Campbell & Salathé, 2013; Christakis & Fowler, 2007; Fowler & Christakis, 2008).

Culture—and the shared knowledge that constitutes it—can be traced in network diagrams. In one such study, Hurtado-de-Mendoza and her associates (2016) were interested in knowing how egocentric networks could offer various forms of psychological resilience for Latina immigrants who suffered from depression or PTSD. These researchers were particularly interested in knowing if these women were able to utilize their existing social networks to mediate or remedy some of these mental health concerns, and what these networks looked like. Previous research looking into networks of immigrant populations showed that they tended to be homogenous/homophilic and centered around family resources, so the present study aimed to verify if this trend was evident in the case at hand, and what impacts this might have on psychological well-being. Following recruitment, participants who met eligibility criteria (immigrant women who suffered from depression or PTSD as a result of trauma) completed a network interview where they described their immediate social relations. Subsequent analyses showed that immigrant women described networks focused primarily around family members, who acted as relevant and vital sources for those women's psychological resiliency. In fact, children and other family members, along with some close friends, comprised the core of many networks described in that study, with emotional support being the most common attribute associated with those ties. Conversely, in that same study, the researchers noted that other forms of support (mainly financial, institutional, or informational) were less important to these groups, highlighting how these resources may not be readily accessible to these immigrant women and thus not reliable sources of support.

OUR LAB: THE DISTINCTIVE NETWORKS OF HIGHLY ENGAGED GAMERS

We wanted to see how intensively involved—potentially "addicted"—internet gamers might exchange ideas about the appropriateness and acceptability of online gaming, and so we developed a personal network study (Dengah, Snodgrass et al., 2018). In particular, we were interested in knowing how notions of homophily—or, by contrast, having a network composed of members whose views on gaming differed from those of the interviewees—could impact our interviewees' psychological states and self-reported "addiction" to online gaming. Our initial hypotheses were twofold. First, we believed that gamers who had networks dominated by other intensively online gamers (thus having highly homophilous networks) would have lower psychological distress, owing to the fact that their gaming habits would be fostered and supported by others. Second, we felt that those possessing networks of higher heterogeneity, dominated by individuals who weren't online gamers, would experience greater distress, due to being in contact with individuals who devalued or denigrated interviewees' passions and interests. Drawing on our own network of gamers, both from our lab sessions and elsewhere, we gathered a group of online gamers together and ran them through egocentric network interviews. Respondents were asked to first provide us the names, familial characteristics, and perceptions on gaming of various important members in their personal networks. In addition, we also asked a series of standard questions to assess our respondents' relative degree of gaming "involvement" (and self-reported "addiction" too). (Figure 8.1 shows a personal network visualization from this study of ours.)

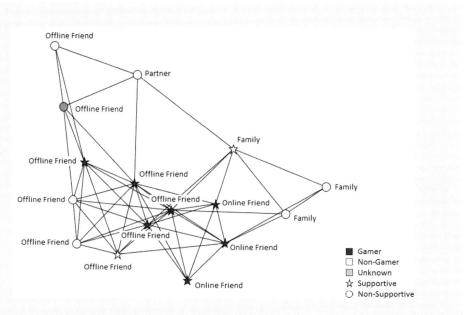

FIGURE 8.1   Gamer Social Network, as Visualized in *EgoNet*.

Our analyses of this data revealed differences between networks that were dominated by online gamers versus those that were not. First and foremost, we confirmed that those surrounded by like-minded individuals reported higher gaming enjoyment. Intuitively, this makes sense: if the important people in your life validate your hobby, and even join in with you, you're more likely to report enjoying gaming. Additionally, we found that individuals with unsupportive networks tended to report gaming in more problematic ways. The explanation for these results could be that the disjunction between the individual and their network makes these gamers feel "stuck" between different worlds and thus different culturally shared models about gaming's acceptability and desirability, resulting in them experiencing greater psychosocial stress and thus reporting more maladaptive/problematic gaming behaviors. The characteristics and makeup of these ego-centric networks also showed some interesting features. The more highly involved gamers in our models had networks dominated by fellow gamers, but these networks were often highly fragmented and composed of simple dyadic (one-to-one) relationships. These networks, while being more supportive of gaming, lacked clear social centers. Why might these networks form? From our ethnographic evidence and surveys, we believe that negative valuations from non-gaming family members or friends led some gamers in our sample to seek out other gamers and form virtual enclaves, which were separated somewhat from interviewees' family, work, etc. ties. This produced more fragmented personal networks, with some networks based primarily on whom our interviewees played with, and others on other criteria.

Big picture: humans are social beings who forge intricate networks of social ties. And research shows that network bonds have direct impacts on physiological and psychological health outcomes. Indeed, the methods described elsewhere in this book all implicitly are shaped by social networks: the responses given to cultural consensus analysis, the types of behavior that manifest as consonance, cultural knowledge is fundamentally shaped by who we socialize with. As we examine these social forces in greater detail, we should remain be cognizant of the ways in which these relationships are formed, maintained, and experienced. By remaining attentive to the dynamic and continually changing webs of connections that connect us as humans, research can further illuminate connections between culture and individual thinking, behavior, and well-being.

SOFTWARE GUIDE: *EGONET*

While we outline here the process of performing personal network analysis using *EgoNet*, there are a number of other networking programs out there that function closely. Programs like *EgoWeb*, *Gephi*, and *Cytoscape* allow researchers to create data visualizations for the kinds of analysis that we describe here, following many of the same basic methodological and analytical principles that we outline here. If you find that *EgoNet* doesn't work the way that you'd like, or are willing to explore other options, give these programs a try. They range in terms of functionality, pricing, and accessibility, but as network analysis has grown into a productive new mode of inquiry, so too have the tools available to researchers interested in investigating social network dynamics.

SOME TERMINOLOGY

Before we begin, we need to cover some terms that are specific to social network analysis (for this discussion, refer to Figure 8.2). An *alter* is an individual within *ego's* (the informant's) social network. When they are graphed, they are also referred to as *nodes*. Alters who know one another are connected by a *tie*. If Bob knows Sally, they are tied together. Ego-centric diagrams are drawn without reference to the informant (this is implied, given that you already establish that the ego knows the alters listed), so only alters are present. Each group of connected/tied alters is called a *component*. Components that are comprised of two tied alters are called *dyad*s, and single

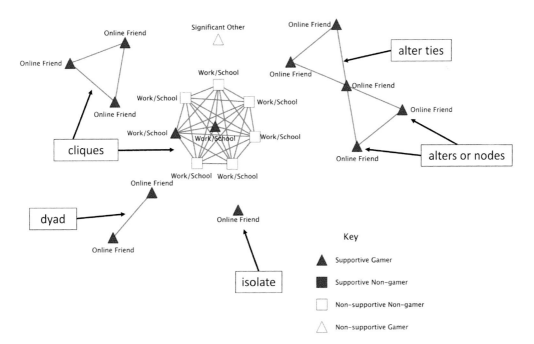

FIGURE 8.2 Social Network Terminology, Visualized in *EgoNet* (adapted from Dengah, Snodgrass, Else, and Pozer 2018).

unconnected alters are called *isolates*. *Cliques* are subgroups of alters where each node is connected to every other node.

DATA COLLECTION

Data collection takes place within *EgoNet* (https://sourceforge.net/projects/*EgoNet*). Currently, no mobile version exists, so interviews will need to include the use of a computer, such as a laptop for the real-time entry of data. It is recommended that the researcher, not the interviewee, input the data. (*EgoWeb* is based on *EgoNet* and has a mobile app (https://www.qualintitative.com/egoweb).)

Opening *EgoNet* will bring a Java-application. There will be two smaller windows ("Interviewing and Analysis Tool" and "Study Design Tool") within a larger application window. The first step it to create an interview protocol in the "Study Design Tool."

- An important note: due to programing quirks in the application, often dialogue boxes will appear small, removing important options from view. Maximize each window while working to avoid missing important options.

STUDY DESIGN TOOL: *EGONET*

This tool will allow you to create the ego-centric social network questionnaire for your study (see Figures 8.3 and 8.4). Click File → New Study. In the pop-up box, name your questionnaire, select "Study Files" from the file type, and click save.

FIGURE 8.3   *EgoNet* Study Design Tool.

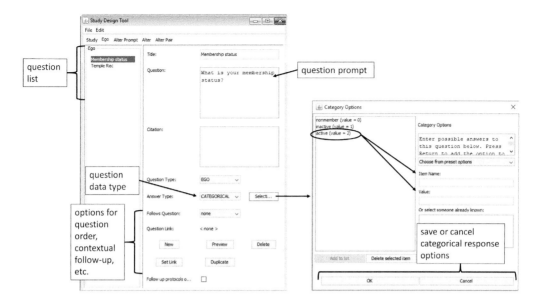

FIGURE 8.4 *EgoNet* Study Design Options.

This will now change the prompt in the "Study Design Tool" box, with a number of different tabs.

STUDY TAB

(1) The first selection is the "Alters numbers mode." This is where you determine the minimum and maximum number of social alters collected from an informant. As a rule of thumb, you generally don't want to go above 20 or so, as the number of alter-alter pairings increases exponentially, increasing informant fatigue. The number of alters, of course, is determined by the research question.

(2) Next, choose how alter names will be entered. Separate first and last names will allow for more organized data, which is especially helpful if one is trying to connect multiple ego social networks via common alters. Keep in mind that in order to combine networks, alters names must be spelled exactly the same, including capitalization.

(3) Alter sampling method: the default option will ask about every possible alter-alter connection. If the research design requires a large number of alters, you can limit the number of alter-alter queries.

EGO TAB

Here, one can create questions related to the ego, or the specific informant/interviewee.

(1) Towards the bottom of the screen, select "New" to create a new question. The Title box (at the top) should highlight, and there will be a new question in the left-handed column under "Ego." This will be the first question in the series. Create a question title, and a question prompt in the text box "Question." "Citation" can be left blank, and in practice is used for researcher reminders to specific question, extrapolations, etc. Don't leave the question prompt box blank, as the titles will not be visible during the actual interview procedure.

(2) Question Type refers to the target category of questions (questions for the ego, alters, and more). Make sure the question type matches the tab name. If this is changed, the question will delete and most buttons on the screen will "gray-out." If this happens, simply select "New" to start the question over again.

(3) For "Answer Type," select the type of data that will be entered as a response to the question. If the response will be categorical, you can create the possible responses via the "selection" button that will appear to the right. Selections will bring up a new dialogue box (be sure to maximize this). Here, you can create categorical responses, and assign a numerical value to each for later analysis. There are a few preset options to choose from or you can add/create your own. In order to add a new response, ensure that no other response option is already highlighted in blue in the left-hand dialogue box—otherwise the new response will write over the existing option. Be sure to click OK after completing the categorical responses.

- Check to make sure the question prompt and responses are accurate via the "Preview" button will open a pop-up box with a preview of the question and responses.

(4) To create more questions, simply select "New" and repeat the procedures. Unless otherwise specified, the questions will follow in the order they were created. This can be changed by highlighting the question in the list to the left, and going to the drop-down box "Follows Question" and selecting the desired preceding question.

- Questions can also be ordered via "if-then" scenarios. After creating the contextual follow-up question, select "Set Link" from the options in the bottom. This will bring up another pop-up box, where you can select the scenario by which the follow-up question will be triggered. Be sure to select "OK" to confirm.

ALTER PROMPT TAB

Most studies will only have one question in this tab (see Figure 8.5). This is the prompt by which you solicit a specific category of social alters from the informant. For example: With whom do you work with? Who are your friends? Whom do you know who smokes?

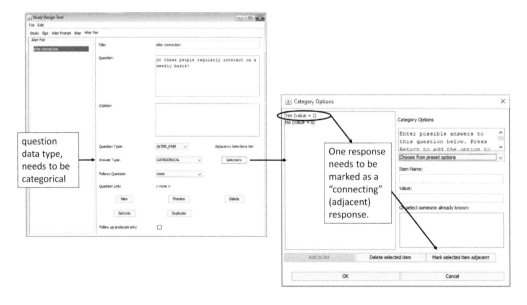

FIGURE 8.5   Alter-alter Connection Prompt, as Seen in *EgoNet*.

Alter tab

The Alter tab collects demographic and similar information about each alter in an ego's network. The question generation procedure is identical to that of the Ego tab.

Alter-pair tab

This set of question prompts will determine the relationship or ties between individuals in the social network. Usually there is only one question to determine alter-alter relationships, though several can be asked. This can be a question like "Do these people work together?" or something like "Would these people interact with one another if you weren't around?" *Be aware that each will multiply the number of alter-alter questions generated.* More than likely, the response will be a categorical "yes/no."

(1) Here, we will need to tell the program which response generates a "tie" between alters. In the "Selections" box (again, maximizing the window will help), highlight in blue the response that will make a connection (most likely "yes"), and then select the button "Mark selected item adjacent."
(2) After "Marking selected item adjacent," the text will turn red. Click OK.
(3) The questionnaire should be complete. Be sure to go to File → Save.

Interviewing and analysis tool

(1) Load the newly created study by clicking on the "Select Study" button and selecting the file created by the Study Design Tool.
(2) To conduct and interview, select the "Start Interview" at the bottom of the window. A new window will pop-up: select "Save or Continue a Respondent Interview (New Respondent)," and save in the created "interview" folder by simply providing a unique file name.
(3) The question prompt will automatically begin. There is an "Interview Notes" tab to take any additional notes required by the study. Note that many users report errors if they select "Previous Question" during the course of the interview. If a change needs to be made, take note as you can make changes to the data upon completion. Upon completion, the data from the interview will automatically be saved in your default "Statistics" folder.

EGOCENTRIC DATA ANALYSIS

(1) You can view each interview by first making sure the proper study is loaded in the Interviewing and Analysis Tool, and then selecting the "View Interview" button, and loading the desired interview (see Figure 8.6).
(2) The Interview tab shows all of the entered data during the interview. If necessary, data may be changed here.
(3) The Statistics tab provides analytical information about the structure of each ego-centric network, including measurements of *centrality* and other structural measures (e.g., *degree* is the count of alter ties for a given node; *closeness* is the inverse sum of distance of an alter to each other alter; *betweenness* is the proportion of shortest network paths a specific alter resides on; *cliques* are a group of maximally interconnected alters; and *components* which are a group of alters connected by at least one tie).

(4) The Graph tab shows a graphical representation of the social network. Here, the diagram can be modified to show demographic and centrality information by changing the shape, size, and color of nodes. And while the nodes can be individually manipulated by dragging and dropping with the mouse, optimized layout configurations can also be selected.

(5) Data for each interview can be downloaded separately by going to File → and selecting one of the various download options. Be aware that some download options will require you to enter a file name to be saved under; select a "Files of type" from the drop-down menu; and manually enter an extension to the file name (e.g., ".jpg").

• Density is a common structural measurement of social networks. It is simply the percentage of all possible ties that are present in a network. Note that density is not automatically calculated in *EgoNet*. This can be done manually by exporting and opening an informant's "Adjacency_Matrix" in *Excel*.

   – In the spreadsheet, calculate the maximum number of possible ties for the network (# of alters = n; $(n^2-n)/2$; this effectually only looks at unique ties between alters, removing redundant ties and meaningless self-ties).

   – Count the number of actual ties. First, delete all redundant data above the diagonal. Next, count the number of ties (value=1); a CTRL-F search can quickly do this.

   – Finally, divide the number of actual ties by the number of possible ties. This is your density value, presented as a %. For example, someone who has 19 ties out of a possible 190 (applicable for someone who has 20 alters), has a network density of 10%.

(6) Finally, returning to the "Interviewing and Analysis Tool" menu, "Save Summary Statistics" will create an excel file with the combined data of all informants in the study. This can be uploaded into a statistical program for other analyses.

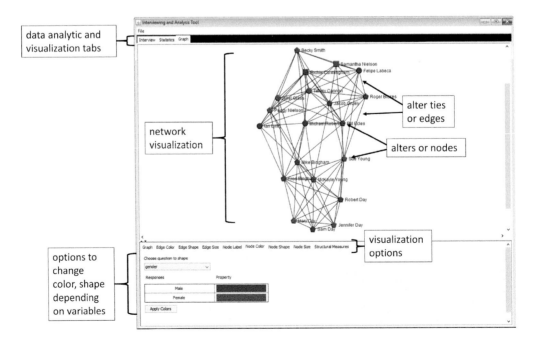

FIGURE 8.6   Visualization of Ego-centric Network in *EgoNet*.

ANALYSES OF AGGREGATE NETWORKS

The aggregate of ego networks can be compiled and analyzed jointly. This is applicable for looking at the entire network of connected and overlapping networks (as in a book club, religious congregation, or other tight-knit community).

(1) After loading the appropriate study in the "Interviewing and Analysis Tool," select the "Whole Network Analysis" button. This will bring up a new box that should be populated with all of the interviews attached to this specific study.

(2) You can manually add or remove interviews via the buttons on the left. Press "Continue."

(3) A new window called "Alter name mapping editor" will appear. This determines how common alters will be linked between the interviews. The default "Settings" allows for alters to appear if mentioned once, includes ego, and ties alters together if at least one informant identifies the alters as connected. "Automatch" will automatically match alters based on common name spellings (in order to manually correct misspellings, you will need to edit the individual interviews as outlined above). Selecting "continue" will generate a graphical representation of the entire network. Specific data files from this can be saved via the Files tab.

EXERCISE: PERSONAL NETWORKS AND TOBACCO/ ALCOHOL USE AND ABUSE

As discussed throughout this chapter, personal network analyses can help researchers better understand the interpersonal relationships constituting any social system—and more specifically, help them see the relationships between an ego and his or her social alters. To better familiarize you with this method's potential, we're going to walk you through some practical personal network exercises using the software *EgoNet*. You will work with a dataset that mirrors in part our videogamer personal networks and gaming involvement/addiction study, which we discussed earlier. But in your practice exercises, you will instead focus on relationships between personal networks and tobacco and alcohol use and abuse.

As in the previous chapter, we divide this chapter's exercises into two parts. In the first part, we'll focus on *EgoNet's* Study Design Tool, walking you through how to create and edit a personal network interview protocol. In the second part, we focus on the Interviewing and Analysis Tool, reviewing some of the basics on visualizing and analyzing your study's data. Also similar to the previous chapter, you will see some overlap in what we said earlier in the chapter and what we describe here in the exercises. We again do that (in large part) intentionally, given the complex nature of this chapter's material as well!

Locate the supplementary datasets for this chapter's practice study: the study is titled, "Ch8_Addiction.ego"; it's accompanied by two separate interviews, "Ch8_Monica.xml" and "Ch8_Manny.xml" (*EgoNet* study files end with the ".ego" suffix, interviews with ".xml"). Save those on your computer.

STUDY DESIGN TOOL EXERCISES

To begin, open the program *EgoNet* and then click on "File/ Open Study" in the Study Design Tool window in order to open this chapter's tobacco and alcohol use/abuse study file ("Ch8_Addiction. ego"). You'll see five tabs at the top (Study, Ego, Alter Prompt, Alter, and Alter Pair), which we'll walk you through individually, each one associated with practices activities.

(1) Study tab: In this tab, you define some of your study's basic parameters, such as the number of each interviewee's alters you'll consider. Remember: in personal network analysis, the study's focus, referred to as ego, is connected to other persons/nodes called alters, who can be variously defined according to the nature of the ego-alter relationship. We might like to collect details on many alters (perhaps even 100s, yeah!), given how that would help us understand better the content and structure of an ego's personal network. However, as mentioned earlier, that is not practical, as it places too much of a response burden on interviewees. Remember, each ego in your study will themselves be listing all their alters and then answering a series of questions about each of them. Then, they'll answer a question (or questions) about every single alter-alter relationship. The latter grows exponentially according to the number of alters in the study. It's thus important to find a middle-ground between having enough alters listed to be meaningful, but not too many so that listing them and their relationships puts too large of a burden on your interviewee (ego). We've found 20 to be a good cut-off mark for the max number of alters in a single study interview. (a) For your first exercise, change the minimum and maximum numbers of alters in this practice study.

(2) Ego tab: This is where you ask the ego (who is the focus of the interview) questions about themselves. You'll see all the questions we've created in this window's left-hand column (e.g., Name, Age, Gender, etc.). For each question you create, you'll need to address: the Question Type (in the Ego tab, questions are by default shown to be "EGO" type queries); the Answer Type (the kind of response data being collected, e.g., CATEGORICAL, NUMERICAL, etc.); and which question this one follows (Follows Question, to set the question order). You also have the ability in this window to "Link" the question that is being edited to some conditional response on a prior question: e.g., we ask further questions about tobacco use (in the Ego:Tobacco_Use_Yes item), but only if respondents answered "yes" to the prior question of whether they used tobacco or not (the Ego:Tobacco_Use question). (a) Create a new question in the Ego tab about ego's race or ethnicity. Name it and list how the question should be asked. Define the Answer Type as CATEGORICAL, and list the possible categorical responses. Have it follow the Ego:Gender question. Click "Preview" to see what your new question looks like. (b) Next, create a new question that is "linked" and thus conditional on one of your race/ethnicity question responses.

(3) Alter Prompt tab: This is where you decide how you'll prompt your interviewee (ego) to list people (alters) with whom they're connected. You'll see we've phrased this study's alter prompt in a rather general "people in your life" sort of way. (a) Change this prompt so that you ask your interviewee to list people associated in some more direct way with their tobacco or alcohol use. (b) Does changing the alter prompt suggest that you should also adjust the minimum and maximum number of requested alters? If so, adjust that phrasing. (c) How do these changes impact the study's focus, and the nature of the data you'd collect?

(4) Alter tab: Here, you ask your interviewee questions about each of the alters they listed in response to the Alter Prompt you just created. Question creation in this tab works in the same way as in the earlier Ego tab. As you'll see, there's again a way to link a question so that it is conditional on the way your respondent answered an earlier question in the alter question items sequence (the Set Link command; the questions again appear in the left column, in the order in which they'll be asked). You'd typically ask your interviewee demographic questions about each alter in their network (age, gender, ethnicity, etc.), as well as questions that advance your understanding of your key study aims, questions, hypotheses, and the like. For example, in this practice study, you'll see that we ask about whether

the interviewee thinks each alter is "addicted" to tobacco/ alcohol or not (Alter:Tobacco_ Addict and Alter:Alcohol_Addict). This is because we anticipate that having a higher percentage of perceived "addicted" individuals in one's personal network might be associated with certain problematic consumption behaviors. Also, the "addicted" alters might interact with each other in particular ways, leading to distinctive personal network structures surrounding ego. (a) Think about a new network hypothesis that you'd like to explore with a new alter question. (b) Create a new alter question relevant to that hypothesis, which you "link" either to an earlier question in the alter item series or to a new question that you create. (c) What do you hope to learn from this new question?

(5) Alter Pair tab: In this fifth and final section of your study protocol, you address how you'll ask ego about their alters' relationships with each other. You'll see that as in our earlier alter prompt we again ask this alter-pair question in a general way (see the Question box near the top). But there are many other possibilities. For example, you can ask if alters in ego's network: work together, live together, or, more relevant in this context, smoke and/or drink together. Also important in this tab is the "Adjacency Selections Set." There, by clicking on the "Selections" button, you set the conditions for when a tie is drawn between two alters. By default, "Yes" is set to "value = 1," meaning that if ego answers "yes" to the alter-pair prompt (regarding whether a pair of alters interact, live, work, smoke, etc. together), then a network tie exists. However, you can toggle this setting so that when ego answers "no" to the alter-alter question, then a tie is established. For example, you might ask ego if members of an alter pair "like" each other. Adjusting this setting to "No"=1 would establish something like a dislike network. (a) Change the alter-pair prompt so that you ask your respondents something more narrowly related to tobacco/alcohol use. (b) Change the Adjacency Selection Set so that a "no" response to the alter-pair prompt is coded as "1." (c) How do these changes affect the nature of the data collected?

INTERVIEWING AND ANALYSIS TOOLS EXERCISES

For this next set of exercises, go to *EgoNet's* Interviewing and Analysis Tool window, where you'll view each of the two study interviews, first Monica's and then Manny's ("Ch8_Monica.xml" and "Ch8_Manny.xml"). To begin, load the interview protocol via "Select Study." Note, you will need to use a fresh copy of our practice protocol, *not* the one you altered via the exercise above. Any changes to the protocol make any previous interviews unreadable. Next, click on "View Interview" and select Monica's interview to view.

(6) Start by clicking on the "Interview" tab, which shows how Monica answered each question. (a) What is Monica's age? (b) Does she describe herself as "addicted" to anything? For the moment, we'll skip the "Statistics" tab, returning to it later in the context of Manny's interview. Instead, jump to the "Graph" tab at the top, which visualizes Monica's network. Near the bottom of this window, in a second "Graph" tab, note that you choose different layouts ("Choose Layout") for how the network data is arranged. The "KKLayout" often tends to shape the network into a more legible form. (c) How many distinct groups do you see in Monica's network? (d) In the "Node Color" tab at the bottom, find and select the "Alter:Know_From" question and click "Apply Colors" to apply this filter to the network. (Remember, expand the window if necessary!) Does this reveal anything about Monica's network's groupings? (e) Repeat this process, but this time use the "Alter:Tobacco_Use" question. Does this reveal anything of interest?

Once those exercises are complete, click "File/ Return to Main Menu" to load a new interview.

(7) Now, let's examine Manny's network interview. In the "Graph" tab at the bottom, toggle different layouts to get one that is legible. (a) How many alter groupings do you see? (b) In "Node Color" at the bottom, select the "Alter:Know_From" question and click "Apply Colors," as you did with Monica's network. What does this show about Manny's personal network? (c) Repeat this process, but this time use the "Alter:Tobacco_Use" question. Does this reveal anything of interest? (d) Next, do the same thing with the "Alter_Alcohol_Use" question filter. What do you see?

Now, click on the "Statistics" tab at the top of the Interviewing and Analysis Tool window. There's a lot of potential here, and a number of network metrics, which you can learn about in books devoted to personal network analysis (e.g., see McCarty et al., 2019). We'll run you through a few relatively straightforward things, in order to familiarize you with some of *EgoNet's* potential in regard to its statistical output. To begin, let's work from the "Structural Measures" tab. (e) How many "components" are in Manny's network, and what does this mean? (f) How many "cliques," and what does that mean? (g) Who is the most "central" member of Manny's network, and how is that significant? Now, click on the "Compositional Summary" tab. (h) What is the average age of alters in Manny's network? (i) The gender composition? Finally, note that in the "Statistics" tab there are other ways to look at each alter's individual data: e.g., in the Degree Centrality, Closeness Centrality, and Betweenness Centrality tabs. But we'll leave you to explore those on your own!

CONCLUSION: CULTURE IN WEBS OF RELATIONSHIPS

Social network analysis can prove to be a powerful tool in the repertoire of social scientists. It can be particularly revealing to trace out how we connect with others in our lives and reflect on how these individuals influence our beliefs, actions, and conceptualizations of culture. Just as Geertz described how "man is an animal suspended in webs of meaning of significance he himself has spun" (Geertz, 1977), social network analysis can help describe how our own personal webs of meaning are connected, intertwined, and shaped by the webs of those around us. While we are all the arbiters of our own cultural truths, how we come to these conclusions is oftentimes the result of internal meditations on the meanings of various cultural models, frames, prototypes, schemas, and many other cognitive processes. The webs of significance and meaning that we create ultimately shape how we view and understand culture, but these cognitive processes are not done in isolation. Rather, these cultural constellations are the result of our social networks and forces outside of our own internal monologues, stories, and narratives. We all share and shape the cultural world we inhabit, whether intentionally or not, through our interactions with those around us. Social network analysis gives us the proper lens to see these phenomena.

9 Conclusion

In this book, we have presented a cognitive anthropological approach for assessing cultural knowledge. There has been some discussion of the theoretical foundations of our cultural "models" and "frames" perspective on culture, particularly in Chapters 1 and 2, and in each chapter's introduction. But the real focus has been on practical applications, both in referencing others' and our own research, and in the book's practical software guides and exercises. In the end, we hope that readers will use what they have learned in this book to advance their understandings of the role culture plays in their own various projects.

We have found in our own work that the approach sketched in this book provides researchers with a powerful toolkit for identifying—and quantifying—simpler proxies for more complex sociocultural processes. Focusing on socially transmitted and shared knowledge in discrete "cultural domains," as we've shown throughout the book, provides a way to rigorously and systematically assess the particular dimensions of culture of interest to a given project. The specific techniques—free lists and pile sorts (Chapters 3 and 4), consensus and consonance analysis (Chapters 5 and 6), finding cultural models in texts (Chapter 7)—are the tools in the toolkit. We hope it's clear that these tools can be used to assess cultural knowledge on various levels of complexity—from simple cognitive objects such as schemas, which, as D'Andrade defined them in his 1995 book, can be held in working memory, to more complex models, theories, and even worldviews (D'Andrade, 1995).

Chapter 8 points to the potential for cognitive anthropological approaches to culture as knowledge to be joined to personal network research. Though not associated with canonical cognitive anthropology, we believe that personal network perspectives are critical to the success of what we have sketched in this book. In the same way that cognitive anthropologists have developed concrete proxies for cultural knowledge, personal network theory locates social structure in specific interpersonal exchanges and relationships. Adding a network perspective ensures that cognitive anthropologists root socially learned knowledge in concrete social interactions, where that knowledge is both acquired and influences others. Methodically, network perspectives force cognitive anthropologists to be more specific about what they mean about culture being socially transmitted and shared— *Transmitted from and shared with whom, and in what context?* Together, cognitive anthropology and personal network research removes "culture" and "society" from the realm of abstract metaphor, so that they can be more precisely measured and assessed in relationship to other processes at play in a given study—be those biological, psychological, environmental, or something else.

After reading this book, we hope that you see the value of sociocognitive methods such as we describe for conducting research from various disciplinary perspectives. We have seen firsthand the strong desire that researchers from other fields—biology and neuroscience, ecology and natural resource management, the health sciences, psychology and psychiatry—have for integrating specifically cultural perspectives into their own work. Ethnography and long-term fieldwork possess perhaps unparalleled power to illuminate local sociocultural processes. But telling someone to go live in a place for several years and study it is less than helpful in solving many of the kinds of research questions posed by our colleagues in other fields. What they more typically need is a way to efficiently identify somewhat discrete (and even quantifiable) proxies for some narrower dimension of culture, which they can integrate into their studies alongside the other variables of concern. This book provides tools to do exactly that.

We also hope that our anthropology audience agrees that the tools we present in this book not only enhance but *are* ethnography. For those unfamiliar with the term, "ethnography" refers to a case study account of a specific group's practices and points of view (Agar, 1980). Historically, ethnographers have relied largely on qualitative interviews (Spradley, 1979) and field-based methods like "participant-observation" (Spradley, 1980). Immersed as participant-observers in naturalistic social settings, ethnographers engage in typically long-term face-to-face interactions with members of a specific group, complementing firsthand experience and self-reflection with more distanced and objective observations of everyday life. We concur that qualitative interview and participatory methods provide effective ways to capture what has been famously referred to as "the native's point of view" (Geertz, 1974). But we think that the cultural domain analysis techniques we present, when used in conjunction with ethnographic methods, can help researchers even more effectively capture local points of view (for a similar idea, see Dressler's (2017, pp. 141–3) discussion of what he calls "emic validity"). The goal of any ethnographer is to faithfully represent the points of view of local community members, as those unfold and are shaped by sociocultural processes. And we have shown how tools like free lists, pile sorts, consensus and consonance analysis, text analysis, and personal network analysis can help researchers do that quite well. Though ethnographers have more typically eschewed numeric thinking, we, following others (e.g., Aunger, 2004; Bernard, 2017; Dressler, 2017; Handwerker, 2001), see no reason why this should be the case. In fact, overcoming the unfortunate biases some researchers in cultural anthropology—and in cultural studies more broadly—demonstrate toward quantification is one of our prime motivations in writing this book, and in promoting instead in our various seminars and talks a "mixed" qualitative-quantitative perspectives. Everything we present in this book is thus entirely compatible, in our opinion, with ethnographic aims and agendas.

To be a bit more specific, ethnographers could use the techniques we describe in these pages to explore more precisely in an initial phase of research the exact content, structure, and sharedness of local knowledge in a specific domain of understanding. Some have even proposed that cultural consensus analysis provides a good way to identify the most culturally knowledgeable individuals (i.e., key-informants), who could be the focus of subsequent in-depth ethnographic interviews (Boster, 1985). Or, researchers might use these methods to confirm in a later research phase something they'd learned earlier via ethnography, such as confirming whether seemingly "cultural" knowledge in a given domain is really shared or not, as well as how that knowledge is variably distributed across individuals and classes of people (Dengah et al., 2019a; Lacy, Snodgrass, Meyer, Dengah, & Benedict, 2018). We thus hope that ethnographers and qualitative researchers will consider integrating some of these perspectives and techniques into their own various research projects, just as we'd encourage quantitative anthropologists and researchers from other fields to turn to participant-observation and long-term fieldwork, if possible within the financial, time, and other constraints of their studies.

Finally, we conclude by saying that we hope this book is viewed as a starting rather than ending point. We have given many examples of cognitive anthropology's potential. But we have certainly not exhausted the ways in which these techniques can be creatively combined with others to illuminate sociocultural processes. As just one example, we believe there is much still to explore in how cognitive anthropology can be combined with personal network research. We would thus direct readers to McCarty's book on personal networks (McCarty, Lubbers, Vacca, & Molina, 2019), which can be read productively alongside our own. Likewise, books broadly surveying cultural anthropological methods of data collection and analysis (e.g., Bernard, 2017) are quite compatible with our more focused consideration of what we have called "sociocognitive" techniques and perspectives. More generally, we would encourage readers to consult the many excellent resources we reference throughout this handbook, in order to extend their knowledge of what we have presented here. Cognitive anthropology is a small field. To survive and flourish, we need additional creative input from scholars in the humanities, as well as from others working in the social, behavioral, and natural sciences. And by this, we mean scholars at all levels in their career—from undergraduate students to senior scientists. We hope you hope you will join us in this exciting enterprise.

Appendix 1
Answer key for chapter exercises

CHAPTER 3: FREE-LISTS

1. (a) *awkward.*
   (b) 3.33.
   (c) It means that on average this item was listed by each respondent about third.
2. (a) Our suggestion for similar terms to lonely: no social life, difficult social life, no friends, no real relationships, isolated, lack of friends, lack of real-life connections. We are tempted to add online friends only to the list. But that opens a can of worms, which may necessitate including, always online. Maybe the online friends are enough to keep one from feeling lonely? Hard to say—look to other forms of ethnographic data for the answer. Based on our research, we would probably group these two in their own "intensive online relationships" category. Also, what about, no social skills? Maybe that goes better with awkward. Again, the "correct" answer depends on the ethnography, the study's analytical goals, and how you want to present the data to readers.
3. (a) Smeeta, with eight items.
   (b) Rashaad had the highest average frequency, 20%.
   (c) This means that Rashaad's items resembled most those in others' lists, with each of his items appearing on average 20% of the time in others' lists.
   (d) Rashaad can be considered a "culture expert" of a kind, with his knowledge of what it means to be an "addicted" gamer reflecting strongly the group's shared ideas or "model."
4. These may vary depending on how you grouped terms for Question 2.
   (a) *awkward* was a term used by all three respondents.
   (b) *angry* was only used by Bethany and Rashaad.
   (c) Smeeta used the terms *unkempt, online friends only, weird, lonely,* and *lack of sleep,* while the others did not.
5. (a) Max had the highest frequency sum of the three, 233.3.
   (b) Max's combination of length of list and average frequency of each item was highest among these three respondents ($7 \times 33.33 = 233.3$).
6. You should have successfully saved this section's work as a .txt file.

CHAPTER 4: PILE-SORTS

1. (a) It's challenging to spot patterns in the Text Data panel, but…
   (b) Items 8 and 4 do appear together frequently in respondents' piles, as do items 2, 3, and 7, and to a certain extent, 10, 20, and 5, which appear together in Ivan's and Rigoberta's piles.
   (c) There are numerous examples of isolates, with item 18, for example, appearing as an isolate in both Mika's and Clarence's piles, and 13 is an isolate in three respondents' piles (Dominique's, Sharon's, and Ivan's). Also note that *Anthropac* shows you that 13 was not sorted ("no pile") for Cathy and Rigoberta—this can alert you to missing or mis-entered data.

2. (a) This is a somewhat subjective process, but you should notice some repeating patterns, e.g., that 8 and 4 are spatially close together, as are 3 and 7 and 10 and 20. Likewise, 18 and 13 do seem somewhat spatially isolated.

   (b) Item 2 seems further away from items 3 and 7 than you might have expected based on the earlier Text Data panel examination, and item 5 seems further from 10 and 20.

3. (a) The emotion term names should have appeared in the Item MDS window, clustered together in ways that should start to make sense to you, e.g., *happy*, *ecstatic*, and *positive* appearing close together, *worthy* and *good enough* spatially close, *satisfied* close to *accomplished*, etc.

4. (a) Emotion terms appear in clusters that should start to make sense to you.

   (b) *Ecstatic* clusters together with *happy*, *positive*, and *warm*.

   (c) Again, ethnography provides many of the answers, but you can see how all these terms signal positive emotional and physiological states, so it makes sense that respondents would group them together.

5. Were you able to successfully change those nodes' appearance?

6. (a) When set at two, a greater number of emotions appear together in each of the two clusters.

   (b) When set at two partitions, the top cluster appears to contain terms that signal positive feelings, while the bottom cluster's terms all relate more narrowly in some way to feeling *accomplished* and thus *satisfied*, *worthy*, etc. Viewing the data set at five partitions provides for more nuanced understandings of conceptual groupings, based on respondents' pile-sorts.

7. (a) Stress: 0.067.

   (b) *Stress* in this instance refers to of how much statistical effort needs to be placed in representing the data spatially in two (or more) dimensions. A lower score means a better fit, a higher score, a worse fit. As a rule of thumb, stress values below 0.15 indicate a good fit (Dugard, Todman, & Staines, 2010, p. 275; see also Sturrock & Rocha, 2000 for a complete table of acceptable stress values for number of sorted items). So, the MDS representation of this emotion data, at 0.067, is acceptable.

8. (a) By viewing the clustering of respondents, you can begin to hypothesize about how respondents appearing in the same cluster might be similar culturally, cognitively, and/or emotionally with one another.

   (b) According to the perspectives presented in this book, we might hypothesize that individuals appearing in the same cluster had been socialized or enculturated in similar ways, which led them to respond emotionally in similar ways to success and failure in their lives.

   (c) By contrast, isolated respondents might have been exposed to different cultural influences, and thus be working from different cultural models about emotional responses to challenging situations.

   (d) This technique might help you identify processes related to cultural learning and thus the transmission of knowledge amongst members of a group (or, by contrast, points of cultural divergence, and the reasons for such divergences).

9. (a) You'll see that group clearly in the center of the screen…

   (b) containing Dominique, Donovan, Mattie, and Sharon.

10. (a) Compared to the larger group, those individuals might possess unique cultural backgrounds, or be in some way unique demographically in terms of their age, education, etc. (or have some combination of unique cultural and demographic background).

    (b) Cathy and Rigoberta might share something in terms of their cultural background and demographics (or, again, some combination of the two).

11. (a) Dominique and Donovan are closest, with the highest agreement (0.889).

(b) Again, their shared cultural background (and/or demographics) may give them a similar perspective on these emotional experiences.

(c) Clarence and Rigoberta correspond the least closely.

(d) 0.621.

(e) They may have different cultural backgrounds, demographically influenced experiences, etc.

12. (a) *Anthropac* tells us that, "Your data exhibit strong fit to the consensus model, supporting an assertion that, despite individual differences, all respondents in the sample belong to a single culture with respect to this domain." Note that you could also average the individual competence scores for this sample, which would be well above 0.5, again consistent with strong cultural sharing.

(b) Yes, respondents seem to be sorting the data in similar ways, which is consistent with the idea that they belong to the same "culture"—at least in regards to this narrow domain of understanding!

13. (a) No single answer here. But overall, the data is consistent with the idea that respondents are sorting material according to a shared (and socially learned) cultural model, with further analysis showing exactly which respondents are most alike. Also, item analysis reveals the structure of this domain of understanding, i.e., exactly which emotions are most closely related to each other, with more fine-grained structure revealed as the number of partitions are increased.

CHAPTER 5: CULTURAL CONSENSUS ANALYSIS

1. There are several ways to open *UCINET's* Spreadsheet, including the graphic button for Matrix Editor found on the toolbar. The *UCINET* Spreadsheet then opens. Within that spreadsheet window, open the *Excel* dataset (that may take a moment!, so be patient), and then save that dataset in the proprietary *UCINET* format (which will add one of those special suffixes).

2. (a) Though using the proprietary *UCINET* software, this appears much like any spreadsheet data, here, with each row corresponding to a *respondent* (R1-R20) and each column to a *variable* (in this instance, terms associated with the Brazilian male gender role, like *provider*, *father*, etc.).

(b) True/false data—that is, respondents said the item either was (true) or was not (false) associated with the male gender role.

(c) Hard to say at this point! But you might note that certain items—like *suffering*—have substantially more 0's than 1's. And *fragile* has *all* zeros. Those might turn out to be highly consensual items (in the "answer key"). Also, respondents differ in their patterns of applying 1's and 0's. For example, R2 and R9 view that the typical Brazilian male avoids alcohol and avoid clubs/bars, contrary to every other respondent. Hence, these individual's "competence score" might end up being low compared to the other respondents.

3. (a) For this data, you're going to want to choose "Covariance model (True/False only)," given the 1/0 (T/F) nature of this dataset.

(b) You would use "Multiple Choice" or "Interval (including ordinal)" if you collected data in those forms.

(c) "Profiles: A row of data for each respondent."

4. (a) First, be sure and save a copy of this output document, wherever it is you are keeping safe and organized the other input and output associated with this study.

(b) You'll note that some respondents have high agreement: e.g., R11 and R15 have an agreement of 0.81, which is quite high! (Here, don't be alarmed if your numbers don't *exactly* match up. *UCINET* may give you slightly different values, depending on the version of the program, different rounding thresholds and other algorithms are used.) In fact, if you check back at the *Excel* or *UCINET* spreadsheets, you will see they agreed on *all* their answers except for three. By contrast, other respondents, such as R2 and R10, have almost nothing in common.

(c) The largest eigenvalue is 9.4. In plain terms, this is a measurement of the amount of variance that can be explained by the first underlying factor derived from this analysis, which is understood to be *shared culture* in the form of the calculated "answer key."

(d) The ratio of the largest to the next largest eigenvalue is over 7. In the tenets of cultural consensus analysis, and as quoted in this text document: "The large eigenratio and the lack of negative competence scores indicates a good fit to the consensus model."

(e) Each respondent's competence score indicates their percentage chance of knowing the culturally shared—and thus "correct"—answer to any of this model's items. Recall that in the cultural consensus framework all items are considered to be of the same level of difficulty. Thus, for example, R1, whose competence is 0.5, has an ~50% chance of knowing the culturally shared or "correct" response for any of the items.

(f) Based on the "answer key," these items were determined to be "true" of societal male gender roles in Brazil: *worker, provider, in-shape, leader, displays wealth, head of household, father, heterosexual, responsible, promiscuous, independent,* and *jealous.* Meanwhile, items such *as avoiding alcohol, avoiding bars/clubs, being religious,* and *being faithful* were not characteristics of the Brazilian man. Overall, the cultural consensus analysis appears to confirm the ethnographic description of Brazilian *machismo*—a family oriented provider and protector, who also gallivants and fraternizes.

5. (a) See supplementary *Excel* file, sheet 3, "Data and Visualization." Note how all the consensus scores cluster between ~+0.4 and +0.9 on the x-axis (loadings on the first factor), suggesting high consensus. Note further the distribution of scores between −0.4 and +0.4 on the y-axis (loadings on the second factor), which shows variation, even within the context of overall consensus. This may suggest the existence of two subcultures.

(b) Compared to the earlier chapter example shown in Figure 5.4, the competence score data (first factor loadings) in the practice sample show a similar high degree of consensus with nearly all the informants clustered along the x-axis. Further, the distribution of informants along the y-axis may suggest subcultural patterns, even within the context of overall cultural agreement (see Appendix 3 for more information).

CHAPTER 6: CULTURAL CONSONANCE ANALYSIS

1. (a) Though focusing on a different cultural domain, the earlier *consensus* exercise asked respondents to respond whether they viewed their culture/society as judging certain items as associated with the model (i.e., whether each item was "true" or "false"). By contrast, in *consonance* analysis, the emphasis is on whether respondents embody each culturally consensual component of involved gaming in their own *personal* thought and behavior.

(b) Though we didn't overly focus in the prior chapter on question framing nuances, we would typically ask respondents in a *consensus* analysis to judge each survey item from the shared "*we*" perspective of their social group (e.g., their gaming guild, gamers in general, etc.) rather than from their own personal point of view. By contrast, in a *consonance* analysis, we're asking respondents whether or not they *personally* enact (in thought and/or behavior) each survey item—that is, from their point of view, whether "I" have each of these involved gaming traits or not (with the response phrased as "true/false," "yes/no," etc.).

2. (a) Rather than a "yes/no" dichotomy, you could employ an ordinal measure such as a Likert rating item in order to assess how much respondents "agreed/disagreed" each of the involved gaming items applied to themselves (on a five or seven or whatever point scale). As another survey strategy, you could also ask how often respondents experienced each of the involved gaming items over some specified time period: e.g., "During the past month, how often did you experience/feel X?" ("Almost never/Once or twice/About once a week/About two to three times a week/Almost every day/Everyday/Many times each day"). There are many possibilities.

   (b) Simple dichotomous ("yes/no") responses might not allow you to meaningfully distinguish between the more and less highly involved gamers.

3. (a) We've calculated respondents' consonance scores in this chapter's *Excel* spreadsheet: see sheet 1's "CONSONANCE SUM" column, which follows the individual involved gamer model items.

4. (a) Depending on your model and your answer key, the culturally "correct" answer for certain items might be a "no" (coded: "0"). You might reverse-code such items—i.e., re-code a "0" as a "1"—when calculating respondents' consonance scores.

   (b) Alternately, you might state such questions in the negative. In this instance, we might know that the culturally correct response for involved gaming (based on earlier consensus analysis) would be "I am *not* awkward," which you might put on your survey phrased this negative way. Then, answering "yes" to this negatively stated question would be the more consonant response, which you could code as "1." But in this instance, changing the question to this negative format doesn't seem very natural.

5. (a) Jeremy scored a 14/15, while Eliza scored a 6/15. Jeremy thus personally embodies in his thought and behavior a large number of features consistent with how the culture defines highly involved videogame play. This indicates that he is highly consonant with the cultural model (and we'd add, he is consonant with the model irrespective of whether he has knowledge of the model, which is a different matter). Eliza, meanwhile, scored relatively low on this model, showing that she doesn't embody many of the characteristics of a highly involved videogame player.

6. (a) From initial observations, there seems to be a pretty clear split between people who scored high on this model (that is, were very consonant with it), and those who scored low.

   (b) Assuming the model accurately assesses gaming involvement, we seem to have a group of highly involved gamers and another of less-involved individuals. In our own research, we've found that some gamers have personally internalized the thinking and behavior associated with highly involved gaming—oftentimes a reflection of their gaming groups' norms—to the extent that such thinking and behavior form a central part of their identity (on cultural internalization, see Maltseva 2015, 2018). It is hard to pinpoint the exact reasons for this, given how identifying centrally as a "gamer" is shaped by a combination of personality traits and social forces, which themselves are in turn influenced by some complex interaction of genetic and environmental factors. Cultural consonance, though an important explanatory factor in many cases, is itself dependent on much else!

7. (a) A cursory observation of the data seems to suggest that individuals reporting higher gaming involvement also demonstrate greater depression.

   (b) It is hard to make definitive claims at this point about the association of these two variables. Assigning causality, of course, would be even trickier. Even if we identified through further analysis a convincing association between these two variables, the causal arrow could go either of two ways: e.g., more highly involved gamers might play in ways that compromise their mental health; or, alternately, depressed individuals might take refuge in highly involved videogame play.

8. (a) beta=0.935. This means that a 1-unit increase in cultural consonance (i.e., answering one more question "yes") is associated with a 0.935 unit increase in depression (i.e., is associated with a change in depression that is almost equivalent to answering another depression symptom question affirmatively).

(b) Yes, this result is highly statistically significant. The p-value is ~0.0005, which is substantially below a conventional threshold of $p \leq 0.05$. This means that if there really was no relationship between depression and consonance scores, the probability is very low that we would get results as strong as this. (Or, more technically, the probability of obtaining these or more extreme results purely by chance is very low, assuming the null hypothesis to be correct (the null hypothesis would be that there is *no* relationship between depression and cultural consonance).)

(c) The explained variance, or R-Squared, is 0.678. The R-Squared provides a model fit statistic that measures how close the data fits the regression line. The closer to 1, the more variance is explained, and the better the model.

(d) This regression model shows that as one becomes more consonant with this cultural model around gaming involvement, depression scores also increase. The beta coefficient gives us a precise estimate of that relationship. The low p-value suggests these results cannot be explained by mere chance. To learn more about using statistics, particularly regressions, for cultural consonance analysis, we refer the reader to Dressler's (2016) book, *The 5 things you need to know about statistics: quantification in ethnographic research.*

Nevertheless, we'd reiterate: identifying an *association* between these two variables is very different than demonstrating a *causal* relationship between them. In our own ethnographic work, we've learned—sometimes the hard way—that one can't rely exclusively on survey data, which can be deceptive, and interpreted in many ways (just as can be true for the reports from ethnographers). For us, ethnographic observations and qualitative interviews continue to centrally inform causal reasoning in our various studies, grounding and contextualizing what we learn through the more formal techniques described in this handbook, which, however powerful, cannot stand alone.

9. (a) See this chapter's supplementary spreadsheet, sheet 3, for that visualization.

(b) For us authors, this corresponds in many respects to how we expected the data to look. However, the visualization does show more clearly how tightly many of the data points cluster around the regression line, as we might have expected given the model's relatively large R-Squared. Finally, we also note that the slope of the regression line appears to be about 1—i.e., moving roughly from consonance scores of 8 to 10 on the x-axis (two units) corresponds to an increase of about 6 to 8 in depression (also two units). This is what we had expected, based on the magnitude of the beta coefficient.

CHAPTER 7: TEXT ANALYSIS

1. (a) The *RoleOfGames/Positive* code was used much more frequently than the *RoleOfGames/Negative* code. You can see this by the size of the squares/nodes in that row. Or, you can click at the top on the "Display nodes as values" icon to represent those as numerical values, which you'll need for the next exercises.

(b & c) RoleOfGames/Positive co-occurs 24 times with the code ResponsesToFailure/Productive/Learn, 16 times with ResponsesToFailure/Productive/Practice, and 10 times with RoleOfGames/GoodQuote.

(d) Among other things, we were interested in this project to quantify whether survey respondents, who were videogame players, tended to respond more *productively* or *detrimentally* to failure, and which kind of *productive/detrimental* responses were judged by respondents to constitute the most *positive/negative* kinds of experiences. Results (a) show that videogames playing a *positive* role in respondents' life was a more salient theme than how those games could play a *negative* role. In (b & c) we see that *learning from one's failures*, as a *positive* role that videogames can play in respondents' lives, is a very salient co-occurring pair of themes in the project, as is the way videogames allow players to *practice failure* and thus learn to handle it better. That is, highly salient positive dimensions of videogames are the way they allow players to "learn" from their mistakes—and thus to "practice" failure, in some sense—and thus ultimately to be better equipped to handle life failures when they invariably occur. We used the *Good Quote* code to flag project quotes that were particularly powerful, which we might want to retrieve later for academic talks, articles, and the like. Here, we identified many (ten) good quotes associated with the positive roles videogames played in respondents' lives, which you could retrieve using the techniques described in this chapter. (Another trick!) We did that, using "Analysis/Complex Coding Query." Here are a few "good quote" excerpts: "I guess one way I've approached this issue is by framing more things as a learning opportunity. Games are great in that they offer (relatively) low-cost consequences to failures: if you mess up, you aren't going to lose your job or your house. That offers you more opportunities to take risks, learn from mistakes, and make the corrections you need to succeed in whatever it is you're doing" (6_EP); "The most profound mentors are loss and defeat" (7_Mediocrates); "Gaming teaches that for repeatable situations you can always try again and get better" (61_Ellie).

2. (a) *Role Of Games/Positive* has a particularly large square/node in 13_Krieger's survey response. Clicking at the top on the "Display nodes as values" icon shows how that code was used three times in 13_Krieger's response. Did you expect the number to be bigger? You can note how that square is three times larger than squares where codes were used just a single time in a document. But looks can be deceiving, as those relative node sizes don't tell you about the actual numbers associated with each node!

(b) The easiest way to determine this is to look at the bottom of the matrix at the "SUM" row. There, you'll see that 21 codes were used to tag text passages in 23_John's survey response, and 17 codes appeared in 13_Krieger's response. Note that these "SUM" cells could represent the fact that a handful of codes—or perhaps even a single code—were frequently used in that document. But here, a variety of codes were employed in each of these two responses.

(c) Look at the far right-hand "SUM" column. There, you'll see that *Role Of Games/ Positive* occurred 42 times across all the documents, and *Responses To Failure/ Productive/Learn* 26 times. Given the prior exercise results, this shouldn't surprise you!

(d) Well, hopefully many things! But we find this visualization exercise useful because it reveals how code occurrences can be unequally distributed across respondents. For example, in an interview project, it's possible that many of that study's coded passages originate from a few—or perhaps even in a single—interview. At the least, some interviewees will be more talkative than others, probably resulting in more coded passages in their interviews, which has implications for how widespread—and thus potentially culturally salient—certain themes are compared to others.

CHAPTER 8: PERSONAL NETWORK ANALYSIS

1. (a) There's no right or wrong answer here. We just want you to start to get comfortable manipulating your study's parameters.

2. (a) The Ego tab is pretty intuitive to use, but you can always review the chapter's earlier guide if you run into problems. Here, you'd first click on the "New" button at the bottom of the Ego tab. That would bring up a new "Ego:Untitled" question in the left-hand column (at the bottom), where all the questions are listed. You name your new variable in the top Title box, e.g., "Ego:Ethnicity" and list how it'd be asked just below that. For question Answer Type, choose "CATEGORICAL" and then click on "Selections." This directs you to a new popup window, where you could enter for Item Name things like: White/Caucasian, Black/African-American, Asian-American, etc. For each, you'd choose a value, 0, 1, 2, and so forth, and then click "Add to list." When you're done with all the options, click "OK." (Remember to expand this and all *EgoNet* popup windows if you can't at first see all the options.) For Follows Question, choose "Ego:Gender," which you'll see moves your new race/ ethnicity question so that it follows gender. The "Preview" button is at the bottom. How does your new question look?

   (b) Again, for guidance, you might look at the way Ego:Tobacco_Use and Ego:Tobacco_ Use_Yes are linked. In any case, you might, for example, decide you want to specify more exactly from where in Asia your Asian-American respondents (egos) originate. First, you'd follow the same procedure as just described for (a): i.e., click on the "New" button to create a new variable, then name it (e.g., "Ego:AsianDescent"), list how to phrase the question, choose again "CATEGORICAL" response type, define the response types (e.g., China, Japan, Vietnam, India, Nepal, whatever you want to add), and for Follows Question choose your race/ethnicity question (e.g., Ego:Ethnicity). The only new thing is that when editing this new variable—e.g., Ego:AsianDescent—you'll click on the "Set Link" button at the bottom of the Ego tab panel. This brings up a popup window, where you'd choose your race/ethnicity question—e.g., Ego:Ethnicity—and then choose, for example, the "Asian-American" response there. The two questions are now linked! Click "Preview" again to see how your new linked question looks.

3. (a) Here, you might specifically ask your respondent to list alters with whom they regularly consume tobacco and/or alcohol (or with whom they don't).

   (b) Among other things, the number of requested alters should be appropriate to your study: e.g., don't ask respondents to list a minimum of 20 drinking buddies, if you anticipate that many of your interviewees wouldn't have so many. If you change this phrasing, make sure you go back to the Study tab and adjust the minimum and maximum alters there!

   (c) There are many possibilities here, based on the specific nature of the changes you made to your study's alter prompt. But asking respondents only for alters with whom they consume tobacco/alcohol means that you won't see how those behaviors occur in their more general personal networks. This could make it harder for you to understand how the tobacco/alcohol consumption behavior impacts (or is impacted by) some of your respondents' primary personal networks. Also, as discussed earlier, raising the minimum/maximum number of alters will give you better network data, but put more of a burden on your interviewee.

4. (a) There are many possibilities here. Perhaps you want to ask ego about each alter's ethnicity, as you think that may inform the content and structure of particular consumption networks surrounding ego. Remember, if you ask a question like this, your interviewee

will give their perception of that, which may differ from how others (even how each alter themselves) would answer the question. Or, you might want to ask some question about each alter's personal or family history of tobacco/alcohol use and/or abuse—their approximate age of first use, if others in their family smoke, drink, etc.—which again might be revealing of ego's network composition and structure. Remember, these questions can be tricky, as your interviewee might not have a good sense of how to answer that for certain alters! That can be okay, if you're interested in ego's perceptions on the matter. But asking such questions can sometimes put your respondent in an uncomfortable position of being asked to report on things they don't know about, which can erode the quality of the interview.

(b) Whatever you decide, follow the same procedure as described in relation to the Ego tab.

(c) We alluded to some possibilities above in our hypothetical new questions. What might you learn from your new questions? The key here is that *every* question should help you advance your research goals. Do not put questions in your protocol that serve no obvious purpose—that will only fatigue your respondent (and you)!

5. (a) As suggested earlier, you could change the alter-pair prompt to something simple, like whether the two alters consume tobacco and/or alcohol with each other.

(b) To do this, click on the "Selections" button. In the popup window, click on "Yes (value = 1)" and type "0" in the value box and then "Add to list." Then, click on "No (value = 0)" and type "1" in its box and then click "Add to list." Click "OK" to accept those changes and exit that window. (Remember, if you don't see some of the options, you may need to maximize this *EgoNet* window.)

(c) The meanings of your data would of course depend on the nature of the changes you made. But if you defined "the two alters do *not* smoke/drink together" as evidence of a network tie, you might conceptualize that as something like a *sobriety*—and perhaps a *support*—network of a kind.

6. (a) Click on "Ego:Ego:Age" in the list to the left. You'll see that Monica is 31.

(b) Click on the "Ego:Ego:Addict_Self" question. No, she does not describe herself as an addict.

(c) In the bottom Graph tab, toggle between the different layout formats, e.g., KKLayout, FRLayout, etc. You should see how Monica's network has three distinct groupings of alters.

(d) You'll see that one group (with Jerome, Martin, and Darrell in it) is a *friend* and *school* group. A second is a *work* group (with Maximo, Janet, etc.). And the third is composed of *family* (Michelle, Albert, etc.).

(e) You'll see that there's tobacco use throughout Monica's network, with some use in each of her three groups, though only Janet uses in Monica's work group.

7. (a) Two groups.

(b) One group is composed exclusively of work colleagues (Freddy, Warren, etc.), the second is a friend and family group.

(c) Most of Manny's alters use tobacco.

(d) Few alters consume alcohol.

(e) Two components. In social network analysis language, a *component* is a maximal set of nodes in which every node can reach every other node via some path. Note that there is no way that Freddy, for example, can reach Alberto—they are thus members of different components. Note that you can click on the "Components" tab (far right) and see the alters in each of them.

(f) Five cliques. A "clique" is a maximal number of actors who have all possible ties present among themselves. But click on the "Cliques" tab to see the alter composition of the five of them. Toggle back-and-forth between those lists and Manny's network visualization, and you'll see how in each case all the members of a given clique have paths connecting them to all the other members of that clique.

(g) Monique, by three different network metrics: degree centrality (the number of ties that a node has, six in Monique's case); closeness centrality (nodes with a high closeness centrality have the shortest distances to all the other nodes); and betweenness centrality (this measures the number of times a node lies on the shortest path between other nodes). Individuals with high centrality measures are likely to be information and resource intermediaries or "brokers" between other individuals in the network. They are often influential people, from a social network point of view!

(h) 36 years old.

(i) 58% male.

Appendix 2
PROFIT (property fitting) analysis

PROFIT analysis stands for Property Fitting analysis. Simply, it allows researchers to determine if the MDS are organized by some a priori (hypothesized) attribute. To successfully perform this analysis, each item will need to have a known continuous/interval or categorical attributes. For example, items may be given attribute data that relate to their degree of importance, gender identity, age, or some other variable. Even the results of constrained pile sorts and cultural consensus can be used as an item attribute.

Dengah and associates' (2019b) examination of racial categories in Brazil can serve as an example of using PROFIT analysis to understand the patterns within an MDS diagram. Building upon previous research (Harris, 1970), Dengah and his team examined racial categories in Brazil, which have been argued to be both organized along a white-black spectrum and ambiguous enough to avoid clear delineation (see Figure A2.1). Using PROFIT analysis, Dengah et al. were able to reassess *raça* (race) distinctions with a pile-sorting activity using facial images of Brazilians. In this activity, these researchers showed participants cards with the faces of Brazilians and asked them to sort them based upon similarities, collecting further data on the features of these piles. Once completed, these piles were then analyzed for similarities, dissimilarities, and categorical features. PROFIT analysis was then performed, helping Dengah and his associates hypothesis test potential categorical criteria that accounted for the distribution pattern of items. This PROFIT analysis revealed that racial distinctions were most strongly structured according to skin color and hair form. Here, what defined someone as being more or less "white," "black," or "mestizo" was a combination of their skin color and hair type (one example being that someone with white skin but kinky hair was seen as being more *sarará* than *branco*). This study thus supported previous findings that *raça* in Brazil could be delineated primarily on a white/black polarity, but that the ambiguities between these poles were structured around skin color and hair type. In using this PROFIT analysis, Dengah and colleagues were thus able to demonstrate that the notion of a Brazilian "racial democracy" (in which racial categorizations were diverse enough to encourage rapid democratization of racial minorities) was tenuous, given the widespread cognitive interpretations of race along this white-black polarity.

PROFIT ANALYSIS

This is a more complicated procedure, as it involves another—though related—program, and importing specific data out of *Visual Anthropac*, and into *UCINET* (Figure A2.2). (You might decide to come back to this later, after gaining some familiarity with *UCINET* routines, described in Chapter 5.)

Important note about *UCINET* #1. *UCINET* will download some outputs to a default folder. At the start of each session, be sure to change the location to the desired folder.

Open *UCINET* → File → Change Default Folder

Important note about *UCINET* #2. Most *UCINET* analyses result in a pop-up text file displaying particular results. These are not automatically saved. Be sure to save this txt file at the end of each analysis manually.

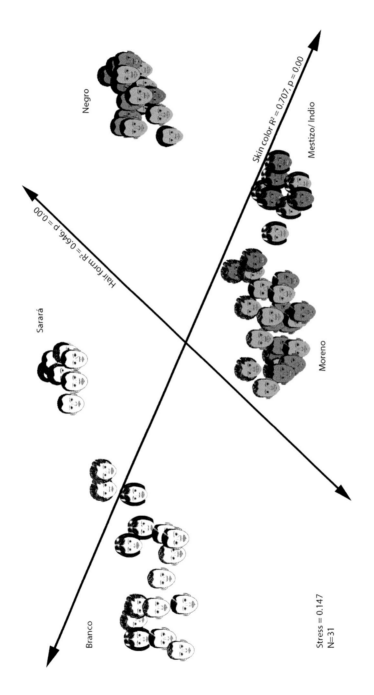

FIGURE A2.1   Multidimensional Scaling (MDS) of 2016 Bahia Data with PROFIT Analysis (from Dengah et al., 2019b).

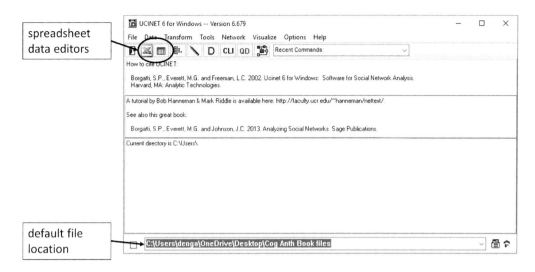

spreadsheet data editors

default file location

FIGURE A2.2 *UCINET* Dashboard.

PROFIT analysis requires two data inputs: (1) The coordinates of the MDS (from *Visual Anthropac*); (2) The attribute data (compiled by the researcher as a separate file).

EXPORT MDS COORDINATES FROM *VISUAL ANTHROPAC*

First, we need to prepare and export our data from *Anthropac*. This can be done in the following way:

1. Items MDS tab → Items → View → Coordinate Matrix
   • This will open a new tab called I-Coord.Matrix.
2. On the I-Coord.Matrix tab, Items → View → Aggregate Proximity Matrix
   • This will open a new tab called I-Agg.Prox.Matrix.
3. File → Export → *UCINET* Matrix Files → Aggregate Proximity Matrix → Save

ATTRIBUTE DATA

Next, prepare you attribute data file, so items contain attribute variables of the hypothesized dimensions. These will need to be dichotomous, interval, or ordinal data. You can create this in any spreadsheet program such as excel. *UCINET* also has its own built-in spreadsheet option.

Each row is a specific item—In the same order as they are entered in the pile sort analysis. So, the term coded as "1" in the pile sort .txt file, should also be the first item in the spreadsheet. Each row is a specific attribute—these will have to be numerically coded (e.g., male =0, female=1).

This data can be entered directly into *UCINET*'s spreadsheet editor, or imported using the directions below:

IMPORT YOUR *EXCEL* ATTRIBUTE FILE

1. Open *UCINET* → Matrix Editor → File → Open your file
   • Your data should be shown in the internal *UCINET* matrix editor (as shown in Figure A2.3).

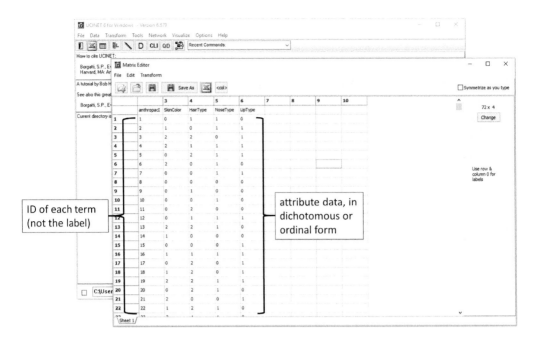

FIGURE A2.3 *UCINET* Spreadsheet Editor for PROFIT Analysis.

• Your item #s and attribute names should be in the grayed vertical and horizontal headings.
2. Save → Make sure you save as a *UCINET* File → Save and close the editor.

IMPORT AGGREGATE DATA FROM *VISUAL ANTHROPAC*

Now, we need to import the aggregate matrix that you already exported from *Visual Anthropac*, and save it in a file form understandable to *UCINET* for Profit Analysis.

1. Back in *UCINET*, go to Tools → Scaling/Decomposition → Non-metric MDS
2. In the pop-up window, perform the following:
   • In INPUT DATASET, select the aggregate proximity matrix file from *Visual Anthropac*.
   • Leave No of dimensions at 2.
   • Similarities selected.
   • Starting Config: Torsca.
   • Starting Config Filename: leave blank.
   • Output dataset: Make sure you save this file in a known location, as we will need this for Profit.
   • Press Okay.

You should receive two new windows, a .txt document (be sure to save manually) with each of the node coordinates, and a stress measure. (Don't worry if the stress or coordinates are slightly different; it is due to the different ways by which these programs conduct MDS.)

The other window will display the graphical representation of the MDS—this should be visually similar to that you created in *Visual Anthropac*. It may not be IDENTICAL, because there is no true North or South, front or back to MDS—so you may be looking at a flipped and inverted representation from the prior one.

PROFIT ANALYSIS

Finally, we are ready to perform PROFIT analysis.

1. *UCINET* → Tools → PROFIT
2. You will get a pop-up window.
   - In the INPUT COORDINATES: select the file you just created for the *UCINET* MDS.
   - For the INPUT ATTRIBUTES: Select the *UCINET* version of your attributes file.
   - Check to make sure the output locations are correct.
   - Leaver the number of permutations at 10,000. Click OK.

RESULTS

You should once again receive two popup windows (Figure A2.4). The first is a .txt file that shows the significance of each proposed attribute. The R-Squared will tell you the amount of variation that is explained by a particular attribute dimension, and the *p*-value will tell you the level of significance. (Be sure to manually save the .txt file.)

You will also receive coordinates for each node, as well as a central coordinate (+) and coordinates for each attribute dimension. To draw dimensions, simply connect a line from the attribute coordinates through the central node.

The second pop up window shows this same information graphically displayed.

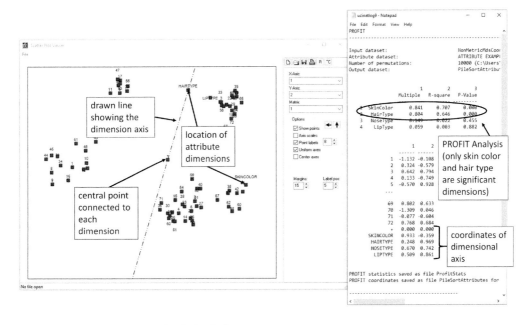

FIGURE A2.4 MDS with PROFIT Analysis.

Appendix 3
Subcultural variation and agreement

The logic behind cultural consensus analysis is that the model tested by the ethnographer is only an approximation of a shared cultural framework. A common misconception is that these methods will, or claim to, uncover a single complete description of culture. Models, by their very definition, are a simplified (or smaller) representation of something. Recent developments, however, are allowing researchers to create even more nuanced models that are fluid and sensitive to intracultural variation. That is, there may be shared knowledge, particularly by a subset of the sample, which is not fully accounted for by the initial model (i.e., answer key). By analyzing subtle patterns in the data, it is possible to understand how members meaningfully deviate from the primary consensus of the aggregate. In mathematical terms, the first factor of cultural consensus analysis explains only part of the underlying variation of the respondent correlation matrix (Weller, 2007). Patterns of residual agreement may lie beyond the overall cultural consensus, indicating subcultural variation or even the existence of an alternative cultural model.

There have been various attempts to look at patterns of variance within cultural consensus analysis (e.g. Boster & Johnson, 1989; Caulkins & Hyatt, 1999; de Munck, Dudley, & Cardinale, 2002; Hruschka, Sibley, Kalim, & Edmonds, 2008; Keller & Loewenstein, 2011; Ross & Medin, 2005). More recent approaches to looking at subcultural variation, or "residual agreement" have been used to look at differences in the "material good life" in Brazil from a ten-year interval (Dressler, Balieiro, & Santos, 2015), and the differences between two Pentecostal congregations' understanding of the ideal religious lifestyle (Dengah, 2013). In each of these, previously identified groups serve as the a priori subgroups to look for deviations away from the shared answer key. These approaches are useful for looking at how two or more known subgroups vary in terms of shared knowledge. However, sometimes knowledge is shared along unknown dimensions. Here, Lacy, Snodgrass, Meyer, Dengah, and Benedict's (2018) contribution becomes helpful. Utilizing an iterative algorithm, Lacy and colleagues wrote a statistical program that randomly separates informants into subgroups in order to maximize the amount of consensus in each. If the consensus in the computer-create subgroups is significantly higher than that of the aggregate, there is evidence of underlying subcultural variation. The researcher would then look at the subgroup membership and the differences in the answer key in order to ascertain the meaning behind these results.

(SUB)CULTURAL VARIATION AND RESIDUAL AGREEMENT ANALYSIS

Cultural consensus describes both the amount of agreement between informants, and the amount of disagreement between informants. By looking for correlations or significant mean differences along the 1st and 2nd factors (usually by a priori demographics), researchers can determine if there is meaningful subcultural patterning of shared knowledge.

If there is meaningful variation along the first factor, this may point to the existence of two or more culturally shared answer keys. That is, the informants may be part of two (or more) different cultural knowledge groups. If there is patterned variation along the second factor, this may suggest subcultural groups, or groups that while sharing cultural knowledge, may have slightly different versions of the model.

There are several different ways of assessing (sub)cultural variation:

METHOD 1

If there is patterned variation along the first factor (by performing a simple correlation between the answer key and a known demographic variable), there is evidence of different answer keys. For this, one can perform separate consensus analysis on each of the subgroups and compare answer keys (ala De Munck et al., 2002; Handwerker & Wozniak, 1997; Hruschka et al., 2008) separately.

METHOD 2

Lacy et al. (2018) also provide a means of looking for multiple answer keys, but without a priori defined subgroups. Via their R and Stata package (https://rdrr.io/cran/SubCultCon/), multiple iterations of individual groupings are created to maximize the eigenvalue ratio of the subgroups. Significantly higher eigenvalue ratios from the aggregate suggest that there are different arrangements of shared knowledge. Researchers can then, a posteriori, look at the meaning behind such groupings.

METHOD 3A

If there is no variation along the first factor, but patterned variation along the second factor (again, by performing a correlation between the second factor scores and a demographic variable), then there is evidence of residual agreement. That is, in the context of overall sharing, there are subtle differences of emphasized knowledge. For true/false and multiple choice data, Dressler et al. (2015) advises to subtract the answer key from each individual's score, and then take the mean deviation of each subgroup. These deviation scores can be plotted along the x- and y-axis, to show differences in emphasis.

METHOD 3B

A similar approach can be taken for ordinal or rank-order data. However, the approach above has the tendency to skew data along the extremes. So instead, Dengah (2014) recommends creating separate answer keys for each subgroup and subtract the aggregate answer key from each. These deviation scores can be plotted and interpreted the same as the approach above (Figure A3.1).

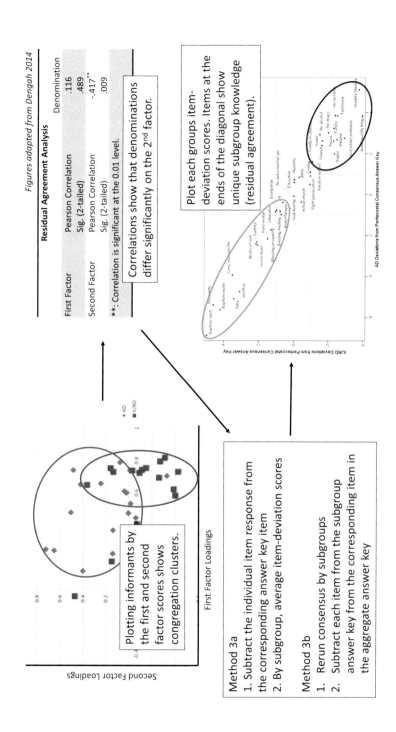

FIGURE A3.1 Residual Agreement (adapted from Dengah 2014).

References

Aarseth, E., Bean, A. M., Boonen, H., Colder Carras, M., Coulson, M., Das, D., ... Van Rooij, A. J. (2016). Scholars' open debate paper on the World Health Organization ICD-11 gaming disorder proposal. *Journal of Behavioral Addictions*, 6(3), 267–70.

Abelson, R. P. (1981). Psychological status of the script concept. *American Psychologist*, 36(7), 715.

Abu-Lughod, L. (2008). Writing against culture. In *The cultural geography reader*. London, UK: Routledge, pp. 62–71.

Adjaye-Gbewonyo, K., & Kawachi, I. (2012). Use of the Yitzhaki Index as a test of relative deprivation for health outcomes: A review of recent literature. *Social Science & Medicine*, 75(1), 129–37.

Adler, N. E., & Ostrove, J. M. (1999). Socioeconomic status and health: What we know and what we don't. *Annals of the New York Academy of Sciences*, 896(1), 3–15.

Agar, M. (1980). *The professional stranger: An informal introduction to ethnography*. New York: Elsevier.

Andrews, C. (2018). *Culture's role in immigrant health: How cultural consonance shapes diabetes and depression among Mexican women in Alabama*. PhD diss., University of Alabama Libraries.

Aral, S., Muchnik, L., & Sundararajan, A. (2009). Distinguishing influence-based contagion from homophily-driven diffusion in dynamic networks. *Proceedings of the National Academy of Sciences*, 106(51), 21544–9.

Atran, S. (1995). Classifying nature across cultures. *Thinking: An Invitation to Cognitive Science*, 3, 131–74.

Atran, S., & Medin, D. L. (2008). *The native mind and the cultural construction of nature*. Cambridge: MIT Press.

Aunger, R. (2004). *Reflexive ethnographic science*. Lanham, MD: Rowman Altamira.

Benedict, R. (1934). *Patterns of culture* (Vol. 8). Boston; New York: Houghton Mifflin Company.

Bennardo, G., & De Munck, V. C. (2014). *Cultural models: Genesis, methods, and experiences*. New York: Oxford University Press.

Bernard, H. R. (2017). *Research methods in anthropology: Qualitative and quantitative approaches* (6th ed.). Lanham, MD: Rowman & Littlefield.

Bernard, H. R., Wutich, A., & Ryan, G. W. (2017). *Analyzing qualitative data: Systematic approaches*. Newbury Park, CA: SAGE publications.

Bessière, K., Seay, A. F., & Kiesler, S. (2007). The ideal elf: Identity exploration in World of Warcraft. *Cyberpsychology & Behavior*, 10(4), 530–5.

Bindon, J. (1997). Coming of age of human adaptability studies in Samoa. In *Human Adaptability: Past, Present, and Future,* S.J. Ulijaszek and R.A. Huss-Ashmore, eds. Oxford, UK: Oxford University Press, pp. 126–156.

Bloch, M. E. F. (1998). *How we think they think: Anthropological approaches to cognition, memory, and literacy*. London, UK: Routledge.

Boellstorff, T., Nardi, B., Pearce, C., & Taylor, T. L. (2012). *Ethnography and virtual worlds: A handbook of method*. Princeton: Princeton University Press.

Borgatti, S. P. (1992). ANTHROPAC version 4.0. *Columbia, South Carolina: Analytic technologies*.

Borgatti, S. P. (1994). Cultural domain analysis. *Journal of Quantitative Anthropology*, 4(4), 261–78.

Borgatti, S. P., Everett, M. G., & Freeman, L. C. (2002). *UCINET for windows: Software for social network analysis*. Harvard, MA: Analytic Technologies

Boster, J. S. (1985). Requiem for the omniscient informant: There's life in the old girl yet. In *Directions in Cognitive Anthropology*, J.W.D. Dougherty, ed. Urbana, IL: University of Illinois Press. pp. 177–97.

Boster, J. S., & Johnson, J. C. (1989). Form or function: A comparison of expert and novice judgments of similarity among fish. *American Anthropologist*, 91(4), 866–89. Retrieved from JSTOR.

Bourdieu, P. (1977). *Outline of a theory of practice* (Vol. 16). Cambridge: Cambridge University Press.

Bourdieu, P. (1984). *Distinction: A social critique of the judgement of taste*. Cambridge: Harvard university press.

Brumann, C. (1999). Writing for culture: Why a successful concept should not be discarded. *Current Anthropology*, 40(S1), S1–S27.

Campbell, E., & Salathé, M. (2013). Complex social contagion makes networks more vulnerable to disease outbreaks. *Scientific Reports*, *3*, 1905.

Caplan, R. D. (1983). Person-environment fit: Past, present, and future. In C. L. Cooper (Ed.), *Stress research* (pp. 35–78). New York: Wiley.

Caplan, R. D., Cobb, S., French, J. R. P., Jr., Harrison, R. V., & Pinneau, S. R. (1980). *Job demands and worker health: Main effects and occupational differences*. Ann Arbor: Institute for Social Research.

Carr, R. L., & Gramling, L. F. (2004). Stigma: A health barrier for women with HIV/AIDS. *The Journal of the Association of Nurses in AIDS Care: JANAC*, *15*(5), 30–9.

Casson, R. W. (1983). Schemata in cognitive anthropology. *Annual Review of Anthropology*, *12*, 429–62.

Caulkins, D., & Hyatt, S. B. (1999). Using consensus analysis to measure cultural diversity in organizations and social movements. *Field Methods*, *11*(1), 5–26.

Chavez, L. R., Hubbell, F. A., McMullin, J. M., Martinez, R. G., & Mishra, S. I. (1995). Understanding knowledge and attitudes about breast cancer: A cultural analysis. *Archives of Family Medicine, 4*(2), 145–152.

Chavez, L. R., McMullin, J. M., Mishra, S. I., & Hubbell, F. A. (2001). Beliefs matter: cultural beliefs and the use of cervical cancer-screening tests. *American Anthropologist*, *103*(4), 1114–29.

Chick, G. (2002). Cultural and behavioral consonance in a Tlaxcalan festival system. *Field Methods*, *14*(1), 26–45.

Chick, G., Dong, E., & Iarmolenko, S. (2014). Cultural consonance in leisure activities and self-rated health in six cities in China. *World Leisure Journal*, *56*(2), 110–19.

Christakis, N. A., & Fowler, J. H. (2007). The spread of obesity in a large social network over 32 years. *New England Journal of Medicine*, *357*(4), 370–9.

Christakis, N. A., & Fowler, J. H. (2013). Social contagion theory: Examining dynamic social networks and human behavior. *Statistics in Medicine*, *32*(4), 556–77.

Cohen, S., & Wills, T. A. (1985). Stress, social support, and the buffering hypothesis. *Psychological Bulletin*, *98*(2), 310–57.

Copeland, T. J. (2011). Poverty, nutrition, and a cultural model of managing HIV/AIDS among women in Nairobi, Kenya. *Annals of Anthropological Practice*, *35*(1), 81–97.

Copeland, T. J., & Dengah, H. J. F. (2016). "Involve me and I learn": Teaching and applying anthropology. *Annals of Anthropological Practice*, *40*(2), 120–33. https://doi.org/10.1111/napa.12096

D'Andrade, R. (1981). The cultural part of cognition. *Cognitive Science*, *5*(3), 179–95.

D'Andrade, R. (1992). Chapter 2: Schemas and motivation. In N. Quinn, D. Fessler, A. W. Johnson, T. S. Lebra, J. Lucy, & H. Whitehead (Eds.), *Human motives and cultural models* (Vol. 1). Cambridge: Cambridge University Press. pp. 23–44.

D'Andrade, R. (1995). *The development of cognitive anthropology*. Cambridge: Cambridge University Press.

D'andrade, R. (2001). A cognitivist's view of the units debate in cultural anthropology. *Cross-cultural Research*, *35*(2), 242–57.

D'Andrade, R. (2005). Some methods for studying cultural cognitive structures. In *Finding culture in talk*, N. Quinn, ed. New York, NY: . Springer. pp. 83–104.

D'Andrade, R. (2006). Commentary on Searle's 'social ontology': Some basic principles' culture and institutions. *Anthropological Theory*, *6*(1), 30–9.

de Munck, V. (2000). *Culture, self, and meaning*. Long Grove, IL: Waveland Press.

de Munck, V. (2020). *Do cultural models exist in the mind or only in publications?* Society for Anthropological Sciences Annual Meeting.

de Munck, V., & Bennardo, G. (2019). Disciplining culture: A sociocognitive approach. *Current Anthropology*, *60*(2), 174–93.

de Munck, V., Dudley, N., & Cardinale, J. (2002). Cultural models of gender in Sri Lanka and the United States. *Ethnology*, *41*(3), 225.

de Saussure, F. (2011). *Course in general linguistics*. New York, NY: Columbia University Press.

Dengah, H. J. F. (2013). The contract with God: Patterns of cultural consensus across two Brazilian religious communities. *Journal of Anthropological Research*, *69*, 347–72.

Dengah, H. J. F. (2014). How religious status shapes psychological well-being: Cultural consonance as a measure of subcultural status among Brazilian Pentecostals. *Social Science & Medicine, 114*, 18–25.

Dengah. H. J. F. (2018). The origins and effects of sociocultural stress: A pilot study on the psychological and physiological outcomes of secular and religious gender role negotiations in urban Brazil. Research Catalyst Grant, Utah State University. ($19,998).

Dengah, H. J. F., Binghman-Thomas, E., Hawvermale, E., & Temple, E. (2019a). "To find that balance:" The impact of cultural consonance and dissonance on mental health among Utah and Mormon women. *Medical Anthropology Quarterly, 33*(3), 439–58.

Dengah, H. J. F., Gilmore, J., Brasileiro, M., Cohen, A. S., Thomas, E. B., Blackburn, J. B., Law, M., Swainston, J., & Thomas, R. (2019b). Cultural models of Raça: The calculus of Brazilian racial identity revisited. *Journal of Anthropological Research, 75*(2), 157–82.

Dengah, H. J. F., Hawvermale, E., Temple, E., Montierth, M., Dutson, T., Young, T., Thomas, E., Patterson, K., Bentley, A., & Tauber, D. (2016). Undergraduates deserve methods too: Using a research laboratory model to engage students in cognitive anthropological research. *Annals of Anthropological Practice, 40*(2), 178–92.

Dengah, H. J. F., & Snodgrass, J. G. (2020). *Avatar* creation in videogaming: Between compensation and constraint. *Games for Health Journal*, May 12, 2020. https://doi.org/10.1089/g4h.2019.0118.

Dengah, H. J. F., Snodgrass, J. G., Else, R. J., & Polzer, E. R. (2018). The social networks and distinctive experiences of intensively involved online gamers: A novel mixed methods approach. *Computers in Human Behavior, 80*, 229–42.

Dressler, W. W. (1996). Culture and blood pressure: Using consensus analysis to create a measurement. *CAM Journal, 8*(3), 6–8.

Dressler, W. W. (2005). What's cultural about biocultural research? *Ethos, 33*(1), 20–45.

Dressler, W. W. (2016). *The 5 things you need to know about statistics: Quantification in ethnographic research.* London, UK: Routledge.

Dressler, W. W. (2017). *Culture and the individual: Theory and method of cultural consonance.* London, UK: Routledge.

Dressler, W. W., Balieiro, M. C., Ribeiro, R. P., & Santos, J. E. D. (2007). Cultural consonance and psychological distress: Examining the associations in multiple cultural domains. *Culture, Medicine and Psychiatry, 31*(2), 195–224.

Dressler, W. W., Balieiro, M. C., Ribeiro, R. P., & Santos, J. E. D. (2009). Cultural consonance, a 5HT2A receptor polymorphism, and depressive symptoms: A longitudinal study of gene × culture interaction in urban Brazil. *American Journal of Human Biology, 21*(1), 91–7.

Dressler, W. W., Balieiro, M. C., & Santos, J. E. D. (1997). The cultural construction of social support in Brazil: Associations with health outcomes." *Culture, Medicine and Psychiatry, 21*(3), 303–35.

Dressler, W. W., Balieiro, M. C., & Santos, J. E. D. (1998). Culture, socioeconomic status, and physical and mental health in Brazil. *Medical Anthropology Quarterly, 12*(4), 424–46.

Dressler, W. W., Balieiro, M. C., & Santos, J. E. D. (2015). Finding culture change in the second factor: Stability and change in cultural consensus and residual agreement. *Field Methods, 27*(1), 22–38.

Dressler, W. W., & Bindon, J. R. (2000). The health consequences of cultural consonance: Cultural dimensions of lifestyle, social support, and arterial blood pressure in an African American community. *American Anthropologist, 102*(2), 244–60.

Dressler, W. W., Dengah, H. J. F., Balieiro, M. C., & Santos, J. E. D. (2013). Cultural consonance, religion and psychological distress in an urban community. *Paidéia (Ribeirão Preto), 23*(55), 151–60.

Dressler, W. W., & Oths, K. S. (2014). Social survey methods. In *Handbook of methods in cultural anthropology, 2nd edition* H.R. Bernard and C.C. Gravlee eds. Lanham, MD: Rowan and Littlefield. pp. 497–515.

Dressler, W. W., Oths, K. S., Balieiro, M. C., Ribeiro, R. P., & Santos, J. E. D. (2012). How culture shapes the body: Cultural consonance and body mass in urban Brazil. *American Journal of human biology: The ifficial Journal of the human biology council, 24*(3), 325–31.

Dressler, W. W., & Santos, J. E. D. (2000). Social and cultural dimensions of hypertension in Brazil: A review. *Cadernos de Saúde Pública, 16*, 303–15.

Duany, J. (2002). *The Puerto Rican nation on the move: Identities on the Island & in the United States.* Chapel Hill, NC: University of North Carolina Press.

Dugard, P., Todman, J., & Staines, H. (2010). *Approaching multivariate analysis: A practical introduction.* London, UK: Routledge/Taylor & Francis Group.

Durkheim, E. ([1897] 1951). *Le suicide: étude de sociologie.* J.A. Spaulding. New York, NY: Free Press.

Edwards, J. R., & Cooper, C. L. (1988). Research in stress, coping, and health: Theoretical and methodological issues1. *Psychological Medicine, 18*(1), 15–20.

Fanany, R., Fanany, I., & Tasady, R. (2014). The experience of old age in West Sumatra, Indonesia: Culture shift and cultural consonance in the modern era. *The International Journal of Aging and Society, 3*(1), 51–9.

Festinger, L. (1954). *A theory of cognitive dissonance*. Stanford: Stanford University Press.

Fowler, J. H., & Christakis, N. A. (2008). Dynamic spread of happiness in a large social network: Longitudinal analysis over 20 years in the Framingham heart study. *BMJ, 337*, a2338.

French, J. R. P., Jr., & Kahn, R. L. (1962). A programmatic approach to studying the industrial environment and mental health. *Journal of Social Issues, 18*, 1–48.

Garcia de Alba, J. E., & Salcedo, A. L. (2002). Beliefs and behaviours for the self care of diabetes mellitus type 2: Study of consensus and applied cultural consonance. In *The Society for Applied Anthropology*. Atlanta, Georgia: 62th Meeting, March 7, 2002

Geertz, C. (1974). "From the native's point of view": On the nature of anthropological understanding. *Bulletin of the American Academy of Arts and Sciences, 28*(1) 26–45.

Geertz, C. (1977). *The interpretation of cultures*. New York: Basic Books.

Geertz, C. (2005). Deep play: Notes on the Balinese cockfight. *Daedalus, 134*(4), 56–86.

Glaser, B. G., & Strauss, A. L. (1967). *The discovery of grounded theory. Strategies for qualitative research*. Chicago, IL: Aldine Publishing Company.

Goodenough, W. H. (1957). *Cultural anthropology and linguistics*. Indianapolis, IN: Bobbs-Merrill.

Goodenough, W. H. (1980). *Description and comparison in cultural anthropology*. Cambridge: Cambridge University Press Archive.

Goodenough, W. H. (1994). Toward a working theory of culture In *Assessing Cultural Anthropology*, R. Borofsky, ed. New York, NY: McGraw Hill. pp. 262–273.

Granovetter, M. S. (1973). The strength of weak ties. *American Journal of Sociology, 78*(6), 1360–80.

Grant, K. L., & Miller, M. L. (2004). A cultural consensus analysis of marine ecological knowledge in the Solomon Islands. *SPC Traditional Marine Resources Management and Knowledge Information Bulletin, 17*, 3–13.

Gravlee, C. C. (2005). Ethnic classification in Southeastern Puerto Rico: The cultural model of "color." *Social Forces, 83*(3), 949–70.

Griffiths, M. D., van Rooij, A. J., Kardefelt-Winther, D., Starcevic, V., Király, O., Pallesen, S., … Demetrovics, Z. (2016). Working towards an international consensus on criteria for assessing internet gaming disorder: A critical commentary on Petry et al. (2016). *Addiction (Abingdon, England), 111*(1), 167–75.

Handwerker, W. P. (2001). *Quick ethnography: A guide to rapid multi-method research*. Walnut Creek: AltaMira.

Handwerker, W. P. (2002). The construct validity of cultures: Cultural diversity, culture theory, and a method for ethnography. *American Anthropologist, 104*(1), 106–22.

Handwerker, W. P., Hatcherson, J., & Herbert, J. (1997). Sampling guidelines for cultural data. *Field Methods, 9*(1), 7–9.

Handwerker, W. P., & Wozniak, D. F. (1997). Sampling strategies for the collection of cultural data: An extension of Boas's answer to Galton's problem. *Current Anthropology, 38*(5), 869–75.

Harris, M. (1970). Referential ambiguity in the calculus of Brazilian racial identity. *Southwestern Journal of Anthropology, 26*(1), 1–14.

Harris, Z. S. (1951). Selected writings of Edward Sapir in language, culture, and personality. *Language, 27*(3), 288–333.

Harrison, R. V. (1978). Person-environment fit and job stress. In C. L. Cooper & R. Payne (Eds.), *Stress at work* (pp. 175–205). New York: Wiley.

Heather, N. (2017). Q: Is addiction a brain disease or a moral failing? A: Neither. *Neuroethics, 10*(1), 115–24.

Henderson, N. L., & Dressler, W. W. (2017). Medical disease or moral defect? Stigma attribution and cultural models of addiction causality in a university population. *Culture, Medicine, and Psychiatry, 41*(4), 480–98.

Hruschka, D. J., Sibley, L. M., Kalim, N., & Edmonds, J. K. (2008). When there is more than one answer key: Cultural theories of postpartum hemorrhage in Matlab, Bangladesh. *Field Methods, 20*(4), 315–37.

Hurtado-de-Mendoza, A., Serrano, A., Gonzales, F. A., Fernandez, N. C., Cabling, M., & Kaltman, S. (2016). Trauma-exposed Latina immigrants' networks: A social network analysis approach. *Journal of Latina/o Psychology, 4*(4), 232–47.

Jakobson, R. (1960). Linguistics and poetics. In *Style in language,*Thomas A. Sebeok, ed.. Cambridge: MIT Press. pp. 350–77.

Johnson, J. C., Weller, S. C., & Brewer, D. D. (2002). Systematic data collection and analysis. *Field Methods, 14*(1), 3–5.

Juul, J. (2013). *The art of failure: An essay on the pain of playing video games.* Cambridge: MIT Press.

Kay, P., & Kempton, W. (1984). What is the Sapir-Whorf hypothesis? *American Anthropologist, 86*(1), 65–79.

Keller, J., & Loewenstein, J. (2011). The cultural category of cooperation: A cultural consensus model analysis for China and the United States. *Organization Science, 22*(2), 299–319.

Keyes, C. L. M. (1998). Social well-being. *Social Psychology Quarterly, 61*(2), 121–40.

Keyes, C. L. M. (2009). *Brief description of the mental health continuum short form (MHC-SF).* Retrieved from https://www.aacu.org/sites/default/files/MHC-SFEnglish.pdf

Kroeber, A. L., & Kluckhohn, C. (1952). *Culture: A critical review of concepts and definitions.* Papers. Peabody Museum of Archaeology & Ethnology, Harvard University.

Kronenfeld, D. B. (2011). Afterword: One cognitive view of culture. In *A Companion to Cognitive Anthropology*, D.B. Kronenfeld, G. Bennardo, V.C. De Munck and M.D. Fischer, eds. Hoboken, NJ: John Wiley and Sons. pp. 569–83.

Kronenfeld, D. B., Bennardo, G., De Munck, V. C., & Fischer, M.D (Eds.). (2015). *A companion to cognitive anthropology.* Hoboken, NJ: John Wiley & Sons.

Kuckartz, U. (2007). *MAXQDA: Qualitative data analysis.* Berlin: VERBI Software.

Lacy, M. G., Snodgrass, J. G., Meyer, M. C., Dengah, H. J. F., & Benedict, N. (2018). A formal method for detecting and describing cultural complexity: Extending classical consensus analysis. *Field Methods, 30*(3), 241–57.

Lakoff, G. (2002). *Moral politics: How liberals and conservatives think.* Chicago: University of Chicago Press.

Lakoff, G. (2014). *The all new don't think of an elephant!: Know your values and frame the debate.* Hartford, VT: Chelsea Green Publishing.

Lévi-Strauss, C. (1969). *The elementary structures of kinship.* Boston, MA: Beacon Press.

Levy, N. (2013). Addiction is not a brain disease (and it matters). *Frontiers in Psychiatry, 4.* https://doi.org/10.3389/fpsyt.2013.00024

Link, B. G., & Phelan, J. C. (2001). Conceptualizing stigma. *Annual Review of Sociology, 27,* 363–85.

Liu, B., Zhang, X., Bussmann, R. W., Hart, R. H., Li, P., Bai, Y., & Long, C. (2016). Garcinia in Southern China: Ethnobotany, management, and niche modeling. *Economic Botany, 70*(4), 416–30.

Lounsbury, F. G., & Goodenough, W. H. (1964). A formal account of the crow-and Omaha-type kinship terminologies. In *explorations in cultural anthropology,* W.H. Goodenough, ed. New York, NY: McGraw-Hill..

Maltseva, K. (2015). Norm internalization and the cognitive mechanism of cultural consonance. *International Journal of Culture and Mental Health, 8*(3), 255–73.

Maltseva, K. (2018). Internalized cultural models, congruity with cultural standards, and mental health. *Journal of Cross-Cultural Psychology, 49*(8), 1302–19.

Marmot, M. G., Stansfeld, S., Patel, C., North, F., Head, J., White, I., … Smith, G. D. (1991). Health inequalities among British civil servants: The Whitehall II study. *The Lancet, 337*(8754), 1387–93.

McCarty, C. (2003). *EgoNet. Personal network software.* Gainesville, FL: University of Florida.

McCarty, C., Lubbers, M. J., Vacca, R., & Molina, J. L. (2019). *Conducting personal network research: A practical guide.* New York, NY: Guilford Press

McGill. (n.d.). FPR-McGill social and cultural neuroscience workshop 2019—FPR. Retrieved May 3, 2019, from https://thefpr.org/fpr-mcgill-social-and-cultural-neuroscience-workshop-2019/

McPherson, M., Smith-Lovin, L., & Cook, J. M. (2001). Birds of a feather: Homophily in social networks. *Annual Review of Sociology, 27,* 415–44.

Mead, M., & Wolfenstein, M. (1955). *Childhood in contemporary cultures* (Vol. 124). Chicago: University of Chicago Press.

Nardi, B. (2010). *My life as a night elf priest.* Ann Arbor: University of Michigan Press.

Paolisso, M., & Maloney, R. S. (2001). Building a constituency for applied environmental anthropology through research. *Practicing Anthropology, 23*(3), 42–6.

Pearl, J., & Mackenzie, D. (2018). *The book of why: The new science of cause and effect.* New York, NY: Basic Books.

Pike, K. L. (1967). Etic and emic standpoints for the description of behavior. In *Language in relation to a unified theory of the structure of human behavior*, K.L. Pike, ed. Berlin, DE: De Gruyter Mouton. (2nd rev. ed., pp. 37–72).

Pincus, T., & Callahan, L. F. (1995). What explains the association between socioeconomic status and health: Primarily access to medical care or mind-body variables? *Advances*, *11*(1), 4–36.

Prance, G. T., Campbell, D. G., & Nelson, B. W. (1977). The ethnobotany of the Paumarí Indians. *Economic Botany*, *31*(2), 129–39.

Quinn, N. (1987). Convergent evidence for a cultural model of American marriage. In *Cultural Models in Language and Thought*, D. Holland ed., 173–92. Cambridge: Cambridge University Press

Quinn, N. (2016). *Finding culture in talk: A collection of methods*. New York, NY: Springer.

Read-Wahidi, M. R. (2014). *A model Guadalupan: Devotion to the virgin of Guadalupe and psychosocial stress among Mexican immigrants*. Tuscaloosa, AL: University of Alabama.

Regier, T., Carstensen, A., & Kemp, C. (2016). Languages support efficient communication about the environment: Words for snow revisited. *PLOS ONE*, *11*(4), e0151138. https://doi.org/10.1371/journal.pone.0151138

Reyes-García, V., Gravlee, C. C., McDade, T. W., Huanca, T., Leonard, W. R., & Tanner, S. (2010). Cultural consonance and psychological well-being. Estimates using longitudinal data from an Amazonian society. *Culture, Medicine, and Psychiatry*, *34*(1), 186–203.

Romney, A. K., Weller, S. C., & Batchelder, W. H. (1986). Culture as consensus: A theory of culture and informant accuracy. *American Anthropologist*, *88*(2), 313–38.

Rosch, E. ([1978] 1999). Principles of categorization (Chapter 8). In *Concepts: Core Readings*, E. Margolis and S. Laurence, eds. Cambridge: MA: MIT Press. pp. 189–206.

Ross, N., & Medin, D. L. (2005). Ethnography and experiments: Cultural models and expertise effects elicited with experimental research techniques. *Field Methods*, *17*(2), 131–49.

Ryan, G. W., & Bernard, H. R. (2003). Techniques to identify themes. *Field Methods*, *15*(1), 85–109.

Sampson, T. D. (2012). *Virality: Contagion theory in the age of networks*. Minneapolis, MN: University of Minnesota Press.

Sapir, E. (1929). The status of linguistics as a science. *Language*, *5*(4), 207.

Sapir, E. (1949). *Selected writings of Edward Sapir in language, culture and personality*. Berkeley, CA: University of California Press.

Sapolsky, R. M. (1998). *Why zebras don't get ulcers—A guide to stress, stress-related disorders and coping*. New York: WH Freeman Publishers.

Saunders, J. B., Hao, W., Long, J., King, D. L., Mann, K., Fauth-Bühler, M., ... Poznyak, V. (2017). Gaming disorder: Its delineation as an important condition for diagnosis, management, and prevention. *Journal of Behavioral Addictions*, *6*(3), 271–9.

Sayles, J. N., Ryan, G. W., Silver, J. S., Sarkisian, C. A., & Cunningham, W. E. (2007). Experiences of social stigma and implications for healthcare among a diverse population of HIV positive adults. *Journal of Urban Health*, *84*(6), 814. https://doi.org/10.1007/s11524-007-9220-4

Schank, R. C., & Abelson, R. P. (1975). Scripts, plans, and knowledge. *IJCAI*, *75*, 151–7.

Schank, R. C., & Abelson, R. P. (1977). *Scripts, plans, goals, and understanding: An inquiry into human knowledge structures*. Hillsdale, New Jersey: Lawrence Erlbaum Associates

Schultz, A. F. (2014). *Biocultural analyses of social status, cultural meaning, and chronic stress among Tsimane' Forager-horticulturalists in Lowland Bolivia and Urban Puerto Ricans*. PhD dissertation, University of Florida.

Singh-Manoux, A., Adler, N. E., & Marmot, M. G. (2003). Subjective social status: Its determinants and its association with measures of ill-health in the Whitehall II study. *Social Science & Medicine*, *56*(6), 1321–33.

Singh-Manoux, A., Marmot, M. G., & Adler, N. E. (2005). Does subjective social status predict health and change in health status better than objective status? *Psychosomatic Medicine*, *67*(6), 855–61.

Smith, C. S., Morris, M., Hill, W., Francovich, C., McMullin, J., Chavez, L., & Rhoads, C. (2004). Cultural consensus analysis as a tool for clinic improvements. *Journal of General Internal Medicine*, *19*(5), 514–8.

Snodgrass, J. G. (2006). *Casting kings: Bards and Indian modernity*. Oxford: Oxford University Press.

Snodgrass, J. G. (2014). Ethnography of online cultures. In *Handbook of Methods in Cultural Anthropology*, *2nd edition*, H.R. Bernard and C.C. Gravlee, eds. Lanham, MD: Rowan and Littlefield. pp. 465–96.

Snodgrass, J. G. (2016). Online virtual worlds as anthropological field sites: Ethnographic methods training via collaborative research of Internet gaming cultures. *Annals of Anthropological Practice, 40*(2), 134–47.

Snodgrass, J. G., Bagwell, A., Patry, J. M., Dengah, H. J. F., Smarr-Foster, C., Van Oostenburg, M., & Lacy, M. G. (2018). The partial truths of compensatory and poor-get-poorer internet use theories: More highly involved videogame players experience greater psychosocial benefits." *Computers in Human Behavior, 78*(Supplement C), 10–25.

Snodgrass, J. G., Batchelder, G., Eisenhauer, S., Howard, L., Dengah, H. J. F., Thompson, R., … Powell, C. (2017). A guild culture of "casual raiding" enhances online gaming experience: A cognitive anthropological and ethnographic approach to world of warcraft. *New Media and Society, 19*(12), 1927–44.

Snodgrass, J. G., Clements, K., Nixon, C., Ortega, C., Lauth, S., & Anderson, M. (2020). An iterative approach to qualitative data analysis: Using theme, cultural models, and content analyses to discover and confirm a grounded theory of how gaming inculcates resilience. *Field Methods, 32*(4), 399–415 In press.

Snodgrass, J. G., Dengah, H. J. F., & Lacy, M. G. (2014). "I swear to God, I only want people here who are losers!" Cultural dissonance and the (problematic) allure of Azeroth. *Medical Anthropology Quarterly, 28*(4), 480–501.

Snodgrass, J. G., Dengah, H. J. F., Lacy, M. G., Bagwell, A., Van Oostenburg, M., & Lende, D. (2017). Online gaming involvement and its positive and negative consequences: A cognitive anthropological "cultural consensus" approach to psychiatric measurement and assessment. *Computers in Human Behavior, 66*, 291–302.

Snodgrass, J. G., Dengah, H. J. F., Lacy, M. G., & Fagan, J. (2011). Cultural consonance and mental wellness in the World of Warcraft: Online games as cognitive technologies of "'absorption-immersion.'" *Cognitive Technology, 16*(1), 11–23.

Snodgrass, J. G., Dengah, H. J. F., Lacy, M. G., & Fagan, J. (2013). A formal anthropological view of motivation models of problematic MMO play: Achievement, social, and immersion factors in the context of culture. *Transcultural Psychiatry, 50*(2), 235–62.

Snodgrass, J. G., Dengah, H. J. F., Lacy, M. G., Fagan, J., Most, D., Blank, M., … Leavitt-Reynolds, A. (2012). Restorative magical adventure or warcrack? Motivated MMO play and the pleasures and perils of online experience. *Games and Culture, 7*(1), 3–28.

Snodgrass, J. G., Dengah, H. J. F., Upadhyay, C., Else, R. J., & Polzer, E. R. (2020). Indian 'Gaming Zones' as oppositional subculture: A norm incongruity 'cultural dissonance' approach to internet gaming pleasure and distress. *Current Anthropology.* In Press.

Snodgrass, J. G., Lacy, M. G., Dengah, H. J. F., & Fagan, J. (2011). Enhancing one life rather than living two: Playing MMOs with offline friends. *Computers in Human Behavior, 27*(3), 1211–22.

Snodgrass, J. G., Lacy, M. G., Sharma, S. K., Jhala, Y. S., Advani, M., Bhargava, N., & Upadhyay, C. (2008). Witch hunts, herbal healing, and discourses of indigenous ecodevelopment in North India: Theory and method in the anthropology of environmentality. *American Anthropologist, 110*(3), 299–312.

Snodgrass, J. G., Lacy, M. G., & Upadhyay, C. (2017). "Developing culturally sensitive affect scales for global mental health research and practice: Emotional balance, not named syndromes, in Indian Adivasi subjective well-being". *Social Science & Medicine (1982), 187*, 174–83.

Spradley, J. P. (1979.) *The ethnographic interview.* New York: Holt, Rinehart, and Winston.

Spradley, J. P. (1980). *Participant-observation.* New York: Holt, Rinehart, and Winston.

Stata Corporation. (2015). *Stata base reference manual release 14.* College Station, Texas: Stata Press

Strauss, C., & Quinn, N. (1993). A cognitive/cultural anthropology. *Assessing Cultural Anthropology,* 284–300.

Strauss, C., & Quinn, N. (1997). *A cognitive theory of cultural meaning* (Vol. 9). Cambridge: Cambridge University Press.

Sturrock, K., & Rocha, J. (2000). A multidimensional scaling stress evaluation table. *Field Methods, 12*(1), 49–60.

Sweet, E. (2010). "If your shoes are raggedy you get talked about": Symbolic and material dimensions of adolescent social status and health. *Social Science & Medicine, 70*(12), 2029–35.

Trubetzkoy, N. S. (1969). *Principles of phonology.* Berkeley and Los Angeles: University of California Press. Translated by Christiane A. M. Baltaxe.

Tylor, E. B. ([1871] 1974). *Primitive culture: Researches into the development of mythology, philosophy, religion, art, and custom.* J. Murray. New Jersey: Gordon Press.

Vivelo, F. R. (1980). Anthropology, applied research, and nonacademic careers: Observations and recommendations, with a personal case history. *Human Organization, 39*(4), 345–57.

Weller, S. C. (2007). Cultural consensus theory: Applications and frequently asked questions. *Field Methods, 19*(4), 339–68.

Weller, S. C., & Romney, A. K. (1988). *Systematic data collection.* Newbury Park, CA: Sage

White, W. L., & Kelly, J. F. (2011). Alcohol/drug/substance "abuse": The history and (hopeful) demise of a pernicious label. *Alcoholism Treatment Quarterly, 29*(3), 317–21.

Wiley, A. S., & Allen, J. S. (2009). *Medical anthropology: A biocultural approach.* Oxford: Oxford University Press.

Wilkinson, R. G. (2000). Inequality and the social environment: A reply to Lynch et al. *Journal of Epidemiology & Community Health, 54*(6), 411–3.

Wilkinson, R. G., & Pickett, K. E. (2007). The problems of relative deprivation: Why some societies do better than others. *Social Science & Medicine, 65*(9), 1965–78.

Yee, N. (2014). *The Proteus paradox: How online games and virtual worlds change us-and how they don't.* New Haven, CT: Yale University Press.

Zank, S., & Hanazaki, N. (2012). Exploring the links between ethnobotany, local therapeutic practices, and protected areas in Santa Catarina coastline, Brazil. *Evidence-Based Complementary and Alternative Medicine, 2012*, 1–15.

Index